ANTHROPOLOGY
AND THE
WILL TO MEANING

Anthropology, Culture and Society

Series Editors:
Professor Thomas Hylland Eriksen, University of Oslo
Dr Katy Gardner, University of Sussex
Dr Jon P. Mitchell, University of Sussex

ANTHROPOLOGY AND THE WILL TO MEANING

A Postcolonial Critique

VASSOS ARGYROU

Pluto Press

LONDON • STERLING, VIRGINIA

First published 2002
by PLUTO PRESS
345 Archway Road, London N6 5AA
and 22883 Quicksilver Drive,
Sterling, VA 20166–2012, USA

www.plutobooks.com

British Library Cataloguing in Publication Data
A catalogue record for this book is available from
the British Library

ISBN 0 7453 1860 6 hardback
ISBN 0 7453 1859 2 paperback

Library of Congress Cataloging in Publication Data
Argyrou, Vassos.
  Anthropology and the will to meaning : a postcolonial critique /
Vassos Argyrou.
    p. cm. — (Anthropology, culture, and society)
  ISBN 0–7453–1860–6 (hardback) — ISBN 0–7453–1859–2 (pbk.)
    1. Anthropology—Philosophy. 2. Ethnology—Philosophy. 3. Meaning
(Philosophy) I. Title. II. Series.
  GN33 .A74 2002
  301'.01—dc21
                                                    2001006764

Reprints: 10   9   8   7   6   5   4   3   2   1   0

Designed and produced for Pluto Press by
Chase Publishing Services, Fortescue, Sidmouth EX10 9QG
Typeset from disk by Stanford DTP Services, Towcester
Printed in the European Union by Antony Rowe, Chippenham, England

CONTENTS

For Michael Herzfeld
με αγάπη και εκτίμηση

1 INTRODUCTION: OF SCHOLARS, GAMBLERS AND THIEVES

This book is about the impossible, if not the impossible in general – for that would be the domain of philosophers – that version of the impossible which manifests itself in ethnological belief and practice.[1] My aim is not merely to designate what this particular impossible is, to provide an account as to why it is impossible, or to outline the different ways in which the discipline and its practitioners have come up against it time and again. It is also, more importantly, to examine why ethnographers should want to imagine, desire and strive to demonstrate the impossible to begin with; and to explain – contrary to those who foresee, foretell or call for an end to anthropology, as the case might be – why ethnographers, having repeatedly grappled with the impossible and failed, must nonetheless persist in their efforts to win a battle that is always already lost.

In ethnological belief and practice, the impossible is the tenet of Sameness. It should not be assumed however that this notion refers to any sort of cultural universalism. On the contrary, Sameness is said to manifest itself, paradoxically enough, in the very cultural diversity that the discipline applauds and celebrates. It refers to the ultimately unworkable idea that despite, or perhaps because of their differences, all societies embody the Same cultural value and worth. It is, in short, the reverse of what ethnographers strive to refute – racism and ethnocentrism.

To say that Sameness is impossible is not to say that it is nothing. Indeed, my intention is not to doubt the existence of the *phenomenon*. Not only do ethnographers imagine and desire Sameness but they also posit it as the only 'real' reality. As I will argue in this study however, although not nothing, Sameness can never manifest itself in the world. Indeed, every attempt to demonstrate that this elusive social condition exists and is real does nothing more than to reproduce its contrary, namely, Otherness, which is to say, difference understood as cultural inferiority. That this is the case should be readily apparent if not on theoretical grounds – about which I shall have more to say in subsequent chapters – certainly in terms of the ethnographer's own historical experience. The discourse that more than any other makes it its business to demonstrate and uphold Sameness is ethnological discourse. If the history of the discipline is anything to go by however, there is not a single ethnological paradigm – whether evolutionism, functionalism, structuralism or culturalism, to name only the major ones – that has not been criticised for dividing the world between West and Other, superior and inferior. There is not even one that has not been found guilty of the ultimate ethnological transgression – ethnocentrism.

Such is the ethnological predicament. It is the unhappy, no doubt, predicament of the ethnographer who struggles (and must struggle) to redeem Otherness only to reproduce it, inadvertently but inevitably, further down the road, time and again. It is a predicament not only because Sameness is impossible but also because the ethnological struggle to attain the unattainable must continue unabated. Ethnographers must persist in their efforts to win a battle always already lost because the alternative would mean nothing less than having to acknowledge the reality of what stands in opposition to Sameness – racism and ethnocentrism. This is not to acknowledge that such profanities exist in the world. It is rather having to recognise that racism and ethnocentrism may be intrinsic to social reality, inescapable facts of the world. Although it is theoretically possible for ethno-graphers to abandon the tenet of Sameness, in practice, and in the absence of an alternative ethical mythology, it would mean nothing less than having to bear the full weight of the world. It would mean having to deal with the crushing realisation that the world is intrinsically ethically arbitrary, absurd and meaningless.

Yet if Sameness is indeed impossible and at the same time an indispens-able ethical myth, something for the ethnographer to hold on to in the void, the ethnological predicament becomes as much, indeed more of a predicament for those on whose behalf the ethnographer's redemptive struggle is undertaken and carried out. For it is they who are always at the receiving end of the ethnographer's discourse, they who must bear the burden of Otherness that the ethnographer's discourse reproduces. What, then, can these Others do to defend themselves against anthropology's humanistic assault? How, in particular, should that Other of sorts, the native who has chosen to become an ethnographer, respond to the discipline's moralising and to the demoralising that it causes? What must I do to keep at bay those whose ambition in life is to save me? How to free myself from a discursive practice which is as obsessed with liberating me as incapable of ever succeeding? In broader terms still, how can I deal with that which everyone born to the Other side of the divide must inevitably, sooner or later, in one way or another confront – Western hegemony? What am I to do to defend myself against the symbolic violence exercised over me by Western definitions of the world, whether these are humanistic and progressive, enlightened and tolerant or otherwise?

The native who has chosen to become an ethnographer is not alone in raising such questions. Nor is he alone in the discursive struggle whose aim is to decentre the West and to open up space for Other ways of thinking and being in the world. There are many others, the Western post-structuralists to begin with, who have opened the way and are leading this struggle –

uncompromising, subversive, vociferously deconstructive; and the post-colonial scholars themselves, in close proximity, in tune and in line with the post-structuralist deconstructive impulses – those 'subaltern' voices that can now speak, are being heard and taken seriously. It would seem, then, that help is close at hand. There is an immense body of critical work to draw from both for inspiration and in terms of choosing the most effective tactics and strategies. What is not at all clear is how far post-structuralists and post-colonial scholars are prepared to go, how far they *can* go and whether 'far' is far enough.

Let me turn first to poststructuralist anthropology. I shall not concern myself with the debate between it and the modernists which, like any other such debate, takes for granted what needs to be questioned and examined in detail. Rather, I shall begin by stating the obvious and in doing so expose both the limits and limitations of so-called 'postmodern anthropology' – what I shall call in this study, for reasons that will soon become apparant, heterodox discourse. The obvious, which is at the same time the best-guarded secret in the discipline, is that there has never been a crisis in ethnological representation, as heterodox ethnographers claim. No such crisis has ever befallen the discipline because the most fundamental ethnological repres-entation – the representation without which there would be no anthropology – is questioned by no one, not least by the heterodox ethnographers themselves. This representation is none other than Sameness. Why this grand but obviously facile claim then?

What is at stake in the heterodox critique of ethnological representation is Sameness itself. Much like any other ethnological paradigm, heterodox discourse strives to uphold Sameness in the face of all those representations of Otherness that contradict and undermine it. Among such representations, not as prominent perhaps, but, for a discipline that makes it its business to uphold Sameness, far more poignant than any which come from outside, are ethnological representations. Hence the cumbersome (because contradic-tory) epistemological critique and the related argument that ethnological representations are 'fictions' and 'partial truths'. This, of course, is not to say all ethnological representations. It is to say, rather, all, *except one*: Sameness. But heterodox ethnographers cannot say this. If they did, they would come face to face with the dreaded question as to why Sameness is excluded from the epistemological critique, why it is not itself fiction and a partial truth. Heterodox ethnographers must therefore remain silent and pretend that there is no contradiction to be dealt with. And the rest of the discipline must go along with the entire charade and pretend to take the heterodox argument seriously – so seriously as to either applaud it or level against it irrelevant criticisms (that it undermines anthropology's scientific status, for instance). Everyone must pretend not to notice what is glaringly obvious. And with good reason. The aim of the discipline, after all, is to uphold Sameness, not to undermine it from within.

Yet the problem – which is both a problem of logical consistency and, more importantly, the problem of Otherness itself – is not resolved by hiding behind Sameness or by hiding Sameness behind facile epistemological arguments. What needs to be explained is not why ethnological representations are fictions and partial truths but rather how, armed as they are with what they posit as the most fundamental truth about Others, ethnographers end up reproducing its contrary. It is understandable that ethnographers – the true natives of anthropology – are not prepared to even raise such a question, let alone address it. As I have already suggested and will discuss in greater detail in subsequent chapters, Sameness is what ethnographers use to hold on to in the void, both sacred and taboo. Yet for those whom anthropology has long turned into natives there can be nothing sacred that crosses the divide. Sameness is a Western ethical myth for ethnological and popular consumption in a social universe where religious myths of the same order have lost their appeal. I – and I do not mean the person but the persona that exists under conditions of Western domination – do not need to treat it as the sacred even if for me, too, it appears as such. I must commit the sacrilege that ethnographers do not dare commit. I have no option but to demythologise it. This is not an easy task undertaken with relish. Western hegemony means being under the spell of Western ideas that appear to the dominated just as rational, meaningful and necessary as they appear to the dominant. The struggle against Western hegemony is a painful process because it is as much a struggle against one's (colonised) self.

I turn to the task of demythologising Sameness in subsequent chapters. For now enough has been said to show that there is nothing in ethnological post-structuralism that can be of use in my own redemptive struggle. If anything, heterodox discourse emerges as an obstacle that stands in my way and has to be removed. But perhaps not everything is lost yet, perhaps help is still close at hand in the form of postcolonial discourse. It is not possible to summarise here such an enormous body of work in a way that does it justice. I shall focus instead on a recent paradigmatic example of postcolonial scholarship, a work whose intentions and strategies are central to the post-colonial project, Dipesh Chakrabarty's (2000) attempt to 'provincialize Europe'.[2]

Despite the grand title – *Provincializing Europe* – the scope of Chakarabarty's book is rather limited. His aim is to repudiate historicism, the idea of a universal human history in which non-Western societies appear to be following in the footsteps of the West – a project, one might add, that has been central in all twentieth-century anthropology. Chakrabarty, then, is not about to mount a comprehensive critique of the West. His project, he is quick to point out, 'does not call for a simplistic, out of hand rejection of modernity, liberal values, universals, science, [or] reason ... ' (2000: 42). On the contrary, as he points out throughout the book and summarises admirably at the end, 'European thought is a gift to us all [non-Europeans]' (2000: 255). It is a gift, Chakrabarty argues, because European thought taught us non-Europeans the values of social justice and equality, even if, as historicism makes abundantly clear, it has never applied these values to the non-West.

The West has always been in the business of teaching the rest of the world values and culture. Is it really necessary to remind Chakrabarty that this 'civilising' mission is otherwise known as the white man's burden? Is it necessary to remind him too that in India certain gifts can be poisonous (Parry 1989) or, in broader terms still, that as Derrida (1992) argues – whom Chakrabarty quotes approvingly – the gift as such is impossible, that it can become a debt and create relations of dependence? It would seem that what may be 'simplistic' is not rejection but rather unthinking acceptance of Western gifts. Indeed, because Chakrabarty and other postcolonial scholars have unthinkingly accepted the 'gifts' borne by the West, their discourse cannot be anything other than a dependent discourse – dependent for authorisation on the powers that be, namely, Western scholars.

Chakrabarty writes subaltern histories and believes that by doing so he can demonstrate the limits of historical thinking and hence make room for Other ways of thinking and being in the world. His point is that history 'is only one among ways of remembering the past' (2000:106) and that the present should be understood as a 'plurality ... lack of totality ... constant fragmentariness' (p. 243), 'as irreducibly not-one' (p. 249). In other words, it should be understood in multi-temporal terms, as a universe that consists of different times (or ways of being) which are irreducible to one another. No doubt, there are Other ways of remembering the past, myth being a para-digmatic example. The question, however, is whether the existence of myth in and of itself can automatically demonstrate the limits of historical thinking. Social justice and equality, which Chakrabarty holds so dear, are also one among other ways of being in the world. If Chakrabarty is not prepared to acknowledge that humanism is limited because of the existence of non-humanism, why should historians acknowledge that their discipline is limited because of the existence of mythical pasts? If he is not prepared to recognise that non-humanistic ways of being are life-ways in their own right that should not be displaced by humanism, why should historians be prepared to recognise subaltern pasts as life-ways in their own right that should not be incorporated by historicism?

Suffice it to say, my intention here is neither to defend history at the expense of mythical thinking nor anti-humanism at the expense of humanism. Rather, it is to highlight the limits of Chakrabarty's own discourse, both its logical and political limits. No doubt, there are many Western scholars who would accept Chakrabarty's argument. The examples that come readily to mind are, first, ethnographers who have themselves been struggling against evolutionism for the most part of the twentieth century and second, post-structuralist scholars. But this would be a self-interested and in a certain sense condescending endorsement, since the postcolonial argument confirms what these scholars have already argued and confirmed themselves. It would be the endorsement of those who have already decided the limits of history in an inaugural and founding act, which is to say, an act that opens up the discursive field in which one can speak about history in this way – an endorsement, in short, that authorises Chakrabarty's own discourse. Such are the political limits of a dependent discourse. If Chakrabarty's book 'provincializes Europe' at all, this is only because Western scholars, or at least some of them, have already decided to 'provincialize' it themselves; the extent to which Europe is provincialised by Chakrabarty's book is the extent delimited and approved by Europe itself; Chakrabarty's provincialisation of Europe is dependent on Europe itself for its effectiveness. This is another way of saying that dependent discourses cannot provincialise Europe. The West remains at the centre of the world even when, or rather because it decides to provincialise itself. It is still the centre precisely because it is *it* that authorises its own 'decentring'.

Any postcolonial attempt to provincialise Europe and decentre the West should indeed aim at demonstrating the limits of history. Postcolonial discourse should also aim at demonstrating the limits of anthropology, sociology, philosophy, of Western discourses in general. Yet it should strive to do so not by writing subaltern histories, native anthropologies, indigenous sociologies or philosophies – not, that is, by writing within the discursive domain opened up and authorised by the powers that be. The aim rather should be to write the history of history, the anthropology of anthropology, the sociology of sociology and the philosophy of philosophy. And if this writing has already been done, say, by post-structuralism, postcolonial discourses should write the post-structuralism of post-structuralism and the metanarrative of metanarratives. And if this too has been done – for in this game 'it's turtles all the way down' or, if one prefers, turtles all the way up – then the meta-metanarrative of any Western metanarrative, all the way down and all the way up. The aim should be to write what the West cannot write if it is to say anything at all, including what any form of Western decon-struction cannot write (for, after all, it too is saying something). Any postcolonial attempt to decentre the West, in short, should write 'unauthor-ised', independent, logically extreme, uncompromisingly subversive discourses. To write like this however, one must be prepared to decline Western 'gifts'. This is not to say that postcolonial scholars should turn native and write nativist discourses. If they did, they would be doing nothing less than to confirm themselves in their pre-assigned inferior status. Native scholars have no option but to play the dominant game. The crucial question is how to play it.

The academic game is the game of knowledge (and ignorance) which is inextricably, if not always intentionally, also a game of power. The only way to put an end to this game (the only way under conditions of domination, that is) is to play it better than the players themselves. The only way to undermine the power of Western definitions of the world that burden the rest of the world is to beat the powers that be at their own game. This is not to say simply win one round of the game. It is to say, rather, play enough or as much as necessary to expose it for what it really is – only a game – a game not because it is innocuous but because it is arbitrary and cannot be grounded anywhere. It is also to say, play and win in such a way as to send the powers that be an unambiguous message: should they wish to play more of this game, it would be at their own risk. By way of illustration, let me turn briefly to a few examples of how games are played and struggles won from the ethnographic area that I know best, the Greek-speaking world.

One of the more interesting characteristics of the area is the agonistic ethos encountered in many communities. Being agonistic is not the same thing as being ant-agonistic. As Peristiany (1965: 188) points out in his study of a Cypriot highland village, a man is agonistic whenever 'his *isotimia*, that is, his right to be treated as a person entitled to equal esteem [is violated]' – for example, when the expatriate who has achieved success in the city returns to the village and treats the local people as inferiors. In general, the villagers studied by Peristiany do not seem to tolerate hierarchical relations of any sort. For even when their *isotimia* is not threatened by other men, there are still other powers to reckon with. 'The Greek [Cypriot] who does not find opponents of honour commensurate with his own pits himself against Fate or the Gods. This is the sin of hubris' (1965: 188). It may well be a sin, but, in such a social universe, a man would not allow even Fate or the Gods to offend his honour. He must challenge them in what can only be described as a metaphysical rebellion.

Peristiany made these observations in 1954 at a time when Cyprus was still a British colony, and, although much has changed since then, there is evidence to suggest that the agonistic ethos of the local people has not disappeared completely.[3] Nonetheless, to understand more fully how this ethos is put into practice, we must turn to another highland village, on another eastern Mediterranean island, the Greek island of Crete, and the work of Michael Herzfeld. In the village of Glendi men engage in agonistic displays that include such practices as the blood feud, bride abduction, the song duel and animal theft.[4] Herzfeld (1985) calls such practices the 'poetics of social interaction'. They are 'poetic' because, much like poetry, which suspends context and focuses on the message for its own sake, their aim is to project difference for its own sake. Projecting difference in this way makes the performer different and distinguishes him from those who are already distinguished. As Herzfeld points out:

in Glendiot idiom, there is less focus on 'being a good man' than on 'being *good at* being a man' – a stance that stresses *performative excellence*. ... Actions that occur at a conventional pace are not noticeable: everyone works hard, most adult males dance elegantly enough, any shepherd can steal a sheep on some occasion or other. What counts is ... effective *movement*. ... The work must be done with flair; the dance executed with new embellishments ... and the [animal] theft must be performed in such a manner that it serves immediate notice on the victim of the perpetrator's skill:

as he is good at stealing, so, too, he will be good at being your enemy or your ally – so choose! (1985: 16)

Glendiot agonistic displays, then, aim at performative excellence but apparently, there are no guarantees that the audience would necessarily judge them as such. Performances often fail to achieve the appropriate impact and as Herzfeld (1985: 18) points out, when they do fail – 'a pointless quarrel' would be an example of failure – local people remark that they 'don't say anything'. If they are deemed successful, on the other hand, they are said to 'say something' and 'to have *simasia*, meaning'. The key seems to be risk. The greater the risk involved, the more meaning is generated; the more daring the undertaking, the greater the admiration for the performer. 'A truly gifted performer may win kudos for sheer nerve, as when he invites policemen to sit down with him to a meal of the meat of the animal he has just stolen' (Herzfeld 1985: 47). Flirting with risk seems to be the basis of the Cypriot highlanders' ideology as well. As Peristiany (1965: 188) points out, for villagers 'a true man is one who is prepared to stake everything on one throw of the dice'.

What sort of meaning, then, do successful agonistic performances generate? What is it that they say which local people find significant? Herzfeld argues that the frequency with which Glendiots use the word *simasia* (meaning) suggests that in their worldview '*nothing* ... can be regarded as subject to fixed definition, nothing ... is certain' (1985: 18). This is an important insight. If nothing is 'fixed' and 'certain', whatever presents itself as immutable, natural and necessary – and in an agonistic, fiercely egalitarian universe that would be above all power – must be exposed for what it is: arbitrary and groundless. Agonistic performances generate meaning and 'say something', then, because they expose in practice the arbitrary nature of power and confirm what the villagers already know. Indeed, they often do so in such playful and, for the powers that be, embarrassing ways, that the audience can only laugh at the grandiose claims of power. Consider, for example, the case of the animal thief who ridicules the police by making them unwitting accomplices to his theft, or the case of the gambler who ridicules Fate by staking everything on one throw of the dice.

The present discourse is inspired by the agonistic ethos of the Cypriot and Cretan highlanders and uses similar tactics. One of its aims is to make the audience laugh at the grandiose claims of Western discursive power – the audience in question being those who are at the receiving end of this form of power. It strives to expose the arbitrary nature of Western power and to remind Others what they already know: that it is naive, to say the least, to think that one small group of societies, in an insignificant part of the world, during an infinitesimal (in the wider scheme of things) time-span has reached such a level of enlightenment as to decide for all of us what it means to Be. It strives to do so by performing according to the rules established by the powers that be themselves, on their home ground, by beating them at their own game. This being a game of knowledge, the aim of this agonistic discourse is to expose the ignorance of the powers that be and self-proclaimed authorities on knowledge. The aim is to show what it is about Others but also, and more importantly, about themselves that ethnographers must remain oblivious to.

Yet this discourse is not only written for the amusement of Others. It is also intended for the benefit of another audience, namely, ethnographers and other Western scholars – the true natives of anthropology. In this case, too, it is inspired by the ethos, and follows closely the unorthodox tactics and 'unauthorised' practices of gamblers and animal thieves.

As Herzfeld points out, the stealing of animals in highland Crete is a symbolic practice. The thief's aim is not to enlarge his flock and to gain power. Rather, the theft is intended to serve as notice to those who already possess large flocks and exercise power. What is at stake, in other words, is the thief's *isotimia*, his right to be treated as a person of equal 'esteem'. This discourse engages in a kind of theft in its own right – the 'stealing' of the discursive logic, methods and conceptual tools of anthropology and, more broadly, of the Western episteme, which it uses to talk about anthropology and the West. Its aim is not to produce more knowledge or to claim the truth for itself but simply to demonstrate what is already known: that judging on the basis of the discursive logic, methods and conceptual tools of the Western episteme, there is no Western discourse – not a single one – that can be grounded anywhere or in anything except in its own arbitrariness. This discourse is also intended to serve as notice to those who claim to be authorities on knowledge and exercise power: there is no Western discourse that cannot be exposed in its groundlessness and arbitrariness, not a single one – including those that expose groundlessness and arbitrariness – that cannot be disenchanted and demythologised. Should the powers that be wish to play more of the game of knowledge and power, it would now be at their own risk.

2 HAS THERE EVER BEEN A CRISIS IN ETHNOLOGICAL REPRESENTATION?

In the aftermath of the heterodox critique of ethnological representation, even the most celebrated ethnographers of orthodox modernity have come to acknowledge that there are epistemological limits to what the discipline's practitioners can know about Others. Geertz (1988: 138), for example, points out that:

> the basic problem [with the current ethnological crisis] is neither the moral uncertainties involved in telling stories about how other people live nor the epistemological one involved in casting those stories in scholarly genres – both of which are real enough, are always there, and go with the territory.

For Geertz, the problem rather is that 'now that such matters are coming to be discussed in the open, rather than covered over with a professional mystique, the burden of authorship seems suddenly heavier'. Nonetheless, Geertz goes on to conclude, this burden 'can, given tenacity enough and courage, be gotten used to'.

That Geertz tries to soften the impact of the heterodox critique by treating the 'epistemological problem' as an old and familiar, even if bothersome ethnological companion is quite understandable. What is significant, however, is not the defensive strategy that Geertz is employing but the fact that he too now feels the need to talk about the problem 'in the open' and to acknowledge that it does indeed exist. There are differences, then, among ethnographers about the gravity of the situation and the importance that one should attach to the problem of ethnological knowledge. With the exception of a few unrelenting positivists, however, there is also general consensus that the problem exists and is 'real enough'.

It is difficult to argue with such unanimity. It is difficult to dissent also because irrespective of what one wishes to do with it, the heterodox argument sounds logical and seems to make sense. Can anyone really deny that ethnographers are socially and historically situated beings? Is it not true that the means which they have at their disposal, namely, representations, are coloured by their social and historical circumstances? And does this not mean that what ethnographers say about Others is not how Others actually are – in-themselves – but as they appear to be from the ethnographer's perspective? In short, is it not the case that the knowledge which the discipline produces is historically contingent, relative and incomplete? It seems that it is, inevitably so.

And yet, when everything is said and done, there is still something left over that does not quite square with the epistemological facts. There is something between the lines of ethnological discourse, unnoticed but highly significant, that flies in the face of such unanimity, that contradicts, and blatantly so, the otherwise airtight heterodox argument. There is one ethnological representation that does not appear to be subject to the ethnographer's historical conditions and conditioning, that tells ethnographers *exactly* how Others are in-themselves, and whose truth *no one* doubts, heterodox ethnographers included. This is not just any representation, say, of kinship or exchange or magic, of this or that tribe, village, town or culture. It is the most fundamental ethnological representation, the condition of possibility of all such particular representations, of every ethnological paradigm, of everything that the discipline has ever said about Others. It is, in short, what makes anthropology possible. This representation that no one in the discipline doubts is Sameness, the reverse of racism and ethnocentrism, the conviction that, however different, strange, or bizarre they may appear, Others are essentially and fundamentally the Same as 'us'.

What is one to make of this representation? If there is an epistemological problem in anthropology, this representation should clearly not exist. But it does exist and acts as the very foundation of the discipline. Hence, there can be no epistemological problem in the discipline. Either this, or the problem that heterodox ethnographers conceptualise in epistemological terms is far more basic and fundamental. Indeed, as I shall try to show in this study, not only is it more basic and fundamental than any problem of knowledge, but it is also far more revealing about the discipline and its practitioners than ethnographers of any persuasion dare to imagine.

THE ETHNOGRAPHER AS 'MAN'

There was a time in the Western intellectual tradition when 'man' – the thinking subject that makes representation and hence knowledge itself the condition of its own possibility – did not exist. Thus argues Foucault (1970) in a book that was to send the epistemological boulder rolling down the hill and into practically every academic field, not least those concerned with the cultivation of tolerance toward Others. At this time, the 'Classical Age' in the history of Western thought, as Foucault labels it, scholars had no epistemological consciousness of themselves. They went about their scholarly tasks using the tools of their trade – representations – with the certainty that the image of the world they constructed was the exact replica of the world as it existed in itself. This is not to say that scholars were blind to the possibility of committing error in the way in which they represented the world; nor is it in fact the case that such representations went undisputed. Indeed, the paradigmatic figure of this period, Descartes, began by doubting everything. The possibility of error, however, was located exclusively in poor crafts-manship, in the misapplication of the tools of the trade. The tools themselves were treated as an inert fact of nature, a given that was unthinkingly taken and confidently employed without any questions being raised about its attributes or origin. In short, scholars assumed – or, to be more precise, had no reason to think otherwise – that representations were neutral and innocent, a transparent medium through which the world manifested itself to the mind undistorted.

Then, Foucault's story continues, 'reflexivity' took over scientific minds.[1] Scholars who represented everything in the world except themselves in the act of representing began to reflect on the nature and conditions of possibility of this cognitive process. Thought finally turned around to face itself and, in this fateful encounter, it finally discovered that it too was a possible object for reflection, something that did not only represent but was also amenable to representation. This discovery, Foucault argues, was a fundamental epistemic event with far-reaching consequences. Under its enormous weight, the 'Classical' episteme finally gave way and modernity emerged as its fateful replacement. It was 'a minuscule but absolutely essential displacement, which toppled the whole of Western thought: representation ha[d] lost the power to provide a foundation' to knowledge (Foucault 1970: 238). For if representation was an object in this world, the product of the human mind rather than the immaculate conception of a transcendental being, by what means and by what right could it claim the privileges of transparency and objectivity? How could it guarantee the truth of knowledge, if, as it was now becoming increasingly apparent, it was itself an object of knowledge with nothing outside it to act as an independent arbitrator and ground? How could representation be something to know with, when at the same time it was itself a thing to be known? Was this not a circularity, a tautology of sorts? Such were the critical questions raised at the end of the 'Classical' era, the gaping holes in the fabric of knowledge that required urgent mending, the patching up of which modernity undertook in haste.

The experience that was taking shape at the end of the eighteenth century, then, was one of increasing uncertainty about the nature of things. Having acquired the truth of their epistemological condition, scholars were now increasingly losing their grip on the truth of the world itself. It was as if the objects of the world, once obligingly open and accessible to the scholarly gaze, were now withdrawing into themselves. Foucault (1970: 239) sketches a picture in which things 'turn in upon themselves, posit their own volumes, and define for themselves an *internal* space' closed off to represen-tation. The truth of things becomes a thing in-itself, an 'architecture they conceal', an 'inaccessible store' from which representation could 'draw out, piece by piece, only tenuous elements whose unity ... always remains hidden'. From the eighteenth century onwards, it would not be 'their identity that beings manifest in representation, but the external relation they establish with the human being' (1970: 313). It would not be knowledge of the essence of things that scholars would acquire in their investigations, but merely knowledge of how things appeared from the outside, not the truth as such of the world, but *a* truth – partial, relative and always uncertain.

The constitution of the scholar as 'man' was the ontological alchemy that brought modernity into being, its most fundamental characteristic and the predicament from which the paradigm has not, and perhaps cannot escape. Not that scholars did not try to stabilise the shaky legs on which the system was standing. Indeed, as Foucault (1970: 303–43) argues, modernity can be defined as precisely that self-defeating and never-ending intellectual struggle to find secure foundations for knowledge. At one end of the spectrum, there are all those strategies that locate the truth of the world in the world itself. But such strategies are unable to explain exactly how this truth is accessed, how it is retrieved, the means by which the gap that separates the subject of knowledge from the object to be known is bridged. The usual appeal to the 'facts' of the world only begs the question since it already presupposes a prior understanding of the world – an understanding, that is, which does not depend on those facts. At the other end of the spectrum, there are those strategies that locate the truth of the world in the scholar's discourse – the discourse that posits truth a priori. But these strategies raise the question as to how one can know in advance the truth of that which is not known and is to be investigated. What is the source of this prior knowledge, if not scholars themselves? And if scholars are the source, how can this knowledge lay claims to objectivity?

Neither the first set of strategies, then, nor the second can provide secure foundation to knowledge – to knowledge in general, and in particular to that domain of investigation concerned with human beings themselves. Indeed, as Foucault (1970: 320) argues, the 'human sciences' are condemned to oscillate between the two extremes, more often than not making use of both strategies and thus ending up being both 'positivist and eschatological'. It is for this reason, according to Foucault, that the 'human sciences' are not, and cannot be, true sciences. The problem with them is not, as it is often suggested, their object of study, which is said to be too dense or elusive. Rather, it is the fact that, in one and the same movement, they posit truth as something independent of the thinking subject and make the thinking subject the condition of possibility of all truth.

One of the first scholars to treat the ethnographer as 'man', insofar at least as he drew attention to the epistemological holes in the discourse that makes Others its object of study, was Edward Said. Said's critique of this discourse draws not only on Foucault but on earlier scholars as well, particularly Gramsci. In many ways, it is also reminiscent of the kind of sociology of knowledge worked out by Mannheim (1936) early in the twentieth century and reiterated more recently, albeit not as radically, by Bourdieu (1977, 1984). Having said that, Said's critique appears in the wake of the

Foucaultian revolution, is in tune with it, and follows, if not the letter, certainly the spirit of Foucault's work.[2]

In his celebrated book, *Orientalism*, Said begins with a postulate that was subsequently to become the hallmark of the heterodox discourse itself. The Orient, Said (1978: 4–5) argues, is not 'an inert fact of nature', a brute reality, something that is 'merely *there*'. No doubt, it is that also, in the sense at least that one can locate in the East various peoples and nations. But beyond this 'brute' fact, there is also discourse about the Orient, which is 'man-made', a human construct, a set of specific representations. The Orient, as a geographical, social or cultural entity, exists in-itself and, to the extent that the people located there are aware of this entity as such an entity, it may exist for-itself as well. For this Orient, Said has very little to say. What he is concerned with is the Orient that exists for others, those who are not a part of this entity but who nonetheless have things to say about it, views to express and judgements to make. In short, he is concerned with the Orient as it exists for Westerners. Said wants to thematise Western discourses about the Orient, to problematise their conditions of possibility, both epistemo-logical and political, and ultimately to question the claims that these discourses lay to the truth of this entity.

To say that the Orient is 'man-made' is already to undermine the repre-sentational validity of the body of knowledge that deals with it. It is to say, in effect, that there is no one to guarantee the truth of representations about the Orient (or about anything else for that matter) except 'man' himself. But 'man' is not God; he is a finite being with limited and incomplete knowledge. He is a historical being, the product of his time and the particular society and culture in which he lives. 'Man's' knowledge, therefore, is not only incomplete but also partial, that is, interested. It reflects, to a lesser or greater extent, the historical circumstances of his society and culture as well as his particular position within them. In short, 'man's' discourse about the Orient is inevitably ideological and political.

Even though Said acknowledges an intellectual debt to Foucault, partic-ularly to the latter's notion of discourse, his line of reasoning is much closer to Mannheim's sociology of knowledge than to Foucault's 'ahistorical', as Habermas (1994) would have it, theory of knowledge and power. Indeed, Said's primary aim is to situate scholars of the Orient within the 'geopolit-ical' entity known as the 'West' and to show how this situatedness accounts both for the relativity of their discourse and its ideological nature. Unlike Foucault, then, and very much like Mannheim, Said is concerned more with the socio-historical and less with the discursive determinants of thought. Indeed, this becomes quite clear in Said's discussion of the distinction between 'pure' and 'political' knowledge.

There is a 'general liberal consensus', according to Said (1978: 10–11), which posits that scholarship produces non-ideological, non-political knowledge. Said finds this consensus highly problematical because, in effect, it places scholars outside society and history. As he points out, however:

no one has ever devised a method for detaching the scholar from the circumstances of life, from the fact of his involvement (conscious or unconscious) with a class, a set of beliefs, a social position, or from the mere activity of being a member of a society.

No one has because no one can; there is simply no such method, no vantage point outside society and history, even for scholars. 'All academic knowledge' is thus 'somehow tinged and impressed with, violated by, the gross political fact' – the fact, that is, of the scholar's inevitable involvement in life. If indeed it is the case, Said (1978: 11) continues:

> that no production of knowledge in the human sciences can ever ignore ... its author's involvement ... in his own circumstances, then it must also be true that for a European or American studying the Orient there can be no disclaiming the main circumstances of *his* actuality.

This actuality is none other than his coming up 'against the Orient as a European or American first, as an individual second'. Knowledge of the Orient, then, is inherently political. It is a social and historical construct, the product of socially and historically situated actors who are unable to see the world through disinterested eyes.

In this way, Said radicalises Mannheim's sociology of knowledge. The latter was able to save the 'purity' of scholarly discourse by defining the ideological in terms of direct involvement in class struggle and the pursuit of economic interests. He could then depict scholars as 'a relatively classless stratum which is not too firmly situated in the social order' (1936: 154) and, by extension, scholarly discourse as relatively independent of collective biases. For Said, by contrast, the question is not only or even mainly the extent to which scholars are involved in class struggles. Beyond purely economic interests, there is the question of cultural interests and cultural concerns; beyond struggles at the material plane, there are struggles at the symbolic level. There is, in short, the question of personal and collective identity, a 'geopolitical awareness' (Said 1978: 12) that divides the world between Orient and Occident, which is as much a formative influence on the scholar's discourse as any economic interest.

This of course is not to say that scholars make no attempt to detach themselves from their circumstances, whether economic, social or cultural. Nor is it in fact the case, Said (1978: 12) argues, that all knowledge is of one piece; 'for there is such a thing as knowledge that is less, rather than more, partial than the individual ... who produces it'. Such knowledge, however, is not 'automatically nonpolitical'. It may be less interested than other kinds of knowledge, but it cannot altogether avoid being implicated in questions of ideology and power.

In anthropology itself, the critique of representation shifts the emphasis from the politics of perception to a politics of presentation. There is, in other words, a shift from the question of how one sees to the question of how one speaks about what one has seen, how one constructs and tells a story to those who were not there. Heterodox ethnographers, then, are primarily

concerned with the circumstances surrounding the production of ethnological discourse and the ways in which ethnographic experience is
transformed into a text. The main argument is that ethnological discourse
is mediated by the fundamental need to tell an effective story – a story that
is coherent, credible and persuasive. Ethnographers must transform ethnographic experience into a well-constructed narrative and do so both by
excluding problematical material and by adopting rhetorical textual
strategies. The end result is little more than a fictional account of the actual
fieldwork encounter.

The fictional character of ethnological discourse becomes apparent when
one compares the experience of fieldwork – the subjective side of things –
with the finished, objectified, rationalised product – the ethnographic text
itself. Ethnographic experience, according to the argument, is unruly, and
fieldwork largely beyond one's immediate control. More often than not,
ethnographers are caught up in situations that they did not plan, do not
grasp and do not know how to deal with. They find themselves in circumstances not of their own choosing and liking that often generate emotions
or lead to acts incompatible with the professional ethos and standards. Ethnographic accounts, by contrast, are authoritative texts – well-organised,
structured, purposeful and confident of themselves. They tell a story in which
ethnographers appear to have been in control throughout their fieldwork
encounters, to have known exactly what they were doing and why, to have
had unlimited patience with, and understanding for the natives. In short,
ethnological texts exclude meticulously whatever is likely to undermine their
authority and legitimacy. As Clifford (1986a: 13) put it, making the general
point, 'states of serious confusion, violent feelings or acts, censorships,
important failures, changes of course, and excessive pleasures' are nowhere
to be found in ethnographic texts.

Such strategies of exclusion have been part and parcel of ethnological
practice from its very beginning. Malinowski, the man who invented
fieldwork, created an authoritative narrative about the Trobrianders by
confining all subjective, 'inappropriate' experience in his personal diary.
Thus, while in the latter Malinowski emerges as a confused subjectivity
plagued by loneliness and uncertainty, as someone highly ambivalent about
the Trobrianders, displaying towards them 'empathy mixed with desire and
aversion' (Clifford 1988c: 110), the persona that appears in *The Argonauts* is
completely different. Here Malinowski is the comprehending, confident,
authoritative ethnographer and the very 'locus of sympathetic understanding' (1988c: 110). For Clifford, the juxtaposition between the diary and *The
Argonauts* is not meant to suggest that the former is the true version of what
went on during Malinowski's fieldwork. The diary is itself a textual account
and therefore another version of the complex, overdetermined encounter
that ethnographers call fieldwork. Rather, the point of the juxtaposition is
to highlight the complexity and irreducibility of such 'unruly' encounters;

it is to make us realise that 'all textual accounts based on fieldwork [are] partial constructions' (Clifford 1988c: 97).

Ethnographic texts are partial, that is, not only incomplete, but also interested constructions for another important reason – their use of rhetorical devices in the process of textualisation. As in the case of exclusion strategies, the most important consideration is buttressing the ethnographer's authority. Thus, special emphasis is given to the ethnographer's 'presence at the event described, his perceptual ability, his "disinterested" perspective, his objectivity, and his sincerity' (Crapanzano 1986: 53; Clifford 1988b). By means of these devices, the ethnographer emerges in the text as someone who not only was 'there' but was also uniquely qualified to do the job. In fact, in some cases, reversal of this strategy – 'a tongue-in-cheek understatement' (Rosaldo 1986: 89) of the ethnographer's knowledge of a people – appears to have the same effect, namely, the shoring up of ethnographic authority. Ethnographers routinely deploy several other textual strategies – the dramatisation of the ethnographer's entrance into the foreign culture (or a particular scene), the use of puns that establish 'a collusive relationship between the ethnographer and ... his readers' (Crapanzano 1986: 69) and a whole host of stylistic, poetic devices that embellish the text and transform dry data into a vivid, lively and entertaining story. All these rhetorical devices are one of the main conditions of possibility of the story's meaningfulness and persuasiveness; they are constitutive of the story itself. Nonetheless, the heterodox argument continues, they receive no such recognition by the ethnographer. There is simply no acknowledgement in the text of the contribution they make to the truth of the story. Rather, the story appears to be based on nothing else but itself, the implicit but untenable assumption being that words carry their entire weight within themselves, that there is only one way to tell the story and therefore no connection between the telling itself and the truth being told.

This, in broad outline, is the heterodox critique of ethnological (re)presentation. Yet, despite the emphasis on textuality and the politics associated with it, heterodox ethnographers return in the end to the more sociologically grounded theme of a politics of perception. This should not be surprising. Over and above any rhetorical strategies that ethnographers employ, what makes a story truly effective is its relevance, the extent to which it addresses current concerns. Indeed, as heterodox ethnographers themselves recognise, the decision to study a particular Other or a certain aspect of Otherness is motivated, albeit mostly unconsciously, by the social and political concerns that ethnographers share with members of their own societies. Thus, stories about Others are in an important sense stories about 'us', indirect or symbolic ways of conversing with the self about the problems that it faces.

Clifford (1986b) provides several examples to demonstrate the allegorical nature of ethnographic writing. Take Mauss, for instance, and his celebrated essay 'The Gift'. The essay was published in 1925 and, according to Clifford, was a response to the breakdown of European reciprocity during the First World War. Mauss wrote about the exchange system of 'archaic' and 'primitive' societies with an eye on the condition of the European societies of his time. In effect, he told a story of generosity, cooperation and reciprocity for his European contemporaries to heed – a story, that is, that held a moral lesson. Or take the work of Margaret Mead and Ruth Benedict. Both responded to the dilemmas that American society faced during the inter- and post-war periods – 'a culture struggling with diverse values, with an apparent breakdown of established traditions, with utopian visions of human malleability and fears of disaggregation' (Clifford 1986b: 102). The rationale in telling such stories to the American public was not merely to further knowledge about Other lives. It was at the same time to suggest ways of dealing with the problems of American life itself. In short, Mead and Benedict understood their work as a largely 'pedagogical, ethical undertaking' (Clifford 1986b: 102).

To say that ethnographic accounts are allegorical is to suggest that the way in which ethnographers perceive Others is shaped by the way they perceive themselves. How they perceive themselves, however, is in turn shaped by their social and historical circumstances. Take feminism, for instance. As Clifford (1986b) rightly points out, this movement explains much of the current ethnological interest in the study of gender and female subjectivity. Feminism is a relatively recent phenomenon and has become possible under determinate social and historical conditions.[3] This new perception and understanding of the self also made visible women of Other societies in a similar light. Thus, it should not be surprising that, for instance, Malinowski had very little to say about Trobriand 'women's productive work', as Weiner (1988) complains, nor that she discovered and made women's work the central theme of her book. Malinowski was in the Trobriand islands during the First World War; Weiner was there in the 1970s at the height of the women's movement. Yet neither Malinowski's 'oversight' nor Weiner's 'discovery' have much to do with textuality and the circumstances surrounding the production of discourse. Rather, they are the result of particular visions made possible by different social and historical circumstances. In this rather roundabout way, then, heterodox ethnographers return to the politics of perception and the kind of radical sociology of knowledge put forward by Said.

Be that as it may, whether one emphasises the politics of perception or the politics of presentation, the critique of ethnological representation leads to one and the same conclusion: ethnographic accounts of Other societies and cultures are 'man-made' constructs, the invention of a rather precocious ethnological imagination, in short, 'fictions' (Clifford 1986a: 6). In its original sense the term 'fiction' refers to things created or fashioned, but in heterodox discourse, it is used to express the more contemporary and far more radical meaning attached to it. As Clifford (1986a: 6) himself explains, in applying the term 'fiction' to ethnographic accounts, 'it is important to preserve the meaning not merely of making, but also of making up, of inventing things not actually real'. To be sure, heterodox ethnographers do not mean to say that Others do not exist. Nor do they mean to say, as some critics have argued, that 'the material world is imaginary and the imaginary world – of pastiche, feathers and newspaper clips – is real' (Polier and Roseberry 1989: 258). For heterodox ethnographers Others are objectively present out there in the world. But, like everything else in the world, they exist in-themselves, as a reality wrapped up in itself, that is, a reality whose truth is forever inaccessible to the ethnographer. What ethnographers invent, then, what is not 'actually real', is not Others as such but Others as they are perceived and presented, that is, (re)presented in ethnological discourse.

Such, then, is the heterodox critique of ethnological (re)presentation. It is a critique that can be, and has been, dismissed as an attack of science and objectivity, as a celebration of extreme relativism and the fragmentation of individual subjectivity, even of nihilism.[4] But such dismissals are surely defensive and counter-productive. They do little more than to reproduce a by now rather stale dichotomy – anthropology as science or art – and block the way to a deeper understanding of heterodox discourse itself and of the discipline in general. What is required to attain such an understanding is serious engagement with heterodox discourse on its own ground.

Heterodox discourse presents itself as an epistemological critique of representation. It is concerned with the limits of ethnological knowledge. It should be apparent, however, that it is itself an epistemological argument, a claim about knowledge and the truth. Heterodox ethnographers claim to know that ethnological knowledge is 'fiction', a 'partial truth'. But how, one might ask, is this knowledge possible? What is it in relation to which ethnological knowledge of Other societies and cultures emerges as 'fiction'? It can only be in relation to the truth, not a partial truth, incomplete and interested, but whole and disinterested – the truth as such. Indeed, the more certain heterodox ethnographers are about the fictional character of ethnological knowledge, the more secure they must be in their knowledge of the truth. But if they do know the truth about Others, there can be no crisis in representation. Either this, or they are caught in the intractable paradox of having to acknowledge that they know what by their own account is unknowable. To explore this paradox further, I will begin once again with a brief reference to Foucault's work.

THE ETHNOLOGICAL REPRESENTATION *PAR EXCELLENCE*

Bentham's panopticon, Foucault (1979) reminds us in his work on discipline and punishment in the modern West, was an architectural structure designed to ensure economical and effective surveillance over prisoners in nineteenth-century England. It was to be – for the plans had never been implemented – an observation tower in the centre of the prison from which the guard could have total visibility of all prison cells. The key to its success, to its economy and effectiveness, was the fact that the guard could see all prisoners at all times but could never be seen by them. Prisoners had to assume that the tower was always manned, that someone was watching them constantly, even if in reality no one did. In effect, the panopticon transformed prisoners into their own guards, forcing them to watch over themselves and behave accordingly in case someone was indeed watching.

For Foucault, the panopticon – not the architectural structure as such but the hidden gaze that establishes a field of total visibility – is the very mechanism by which power is deployed in modern Western societies. The panoptic technique, according to Foucault, has escaped from the prison for which it was first conceived and has found fertile ground in the factory, the hospital, the school and other such organised spaces; its power has penetrated the entire social body.

Foucault's assessment of the nature and extent of power in the modern West is debatable, but my concern here is with the logical grounds of his argument. The panopticon, very much like George Orwell's (1949) Big Brother, is the eye that sees all. This suggests that Foucault must in turn be the eye that watches the panopticon in the process of gazing down upon us. Yet, unlike Orwell who *imagined* Big Brother watching everyone in the imaginary world of Oceania, Foucault is actually situated within the real space that is being watched. How, then, can he be such an all-seeing eye? How can he know that the panopticon weaves the webs of power around modern Western lives if he too is caught up in this web? Foucault claims to know, nonetheless, and is telling the rest of us who know nothing of this predicament – since we are caught within it – that this indeed is the truth of the modern human condition. For this knowledge to be possible at all, however, we must assume that he, unlike the rest of us, has found some way, somehow, to escape this field of total visibility. We must assume, and above all he must acknowledge, that he is speaking to us from a real supra-panoptic position. Otherwise, his argument would be no different from Orwell's total-itarian but fortunately imaginary vision. It would be another work of *fiction* and not, as Foucault clearly intended, a factual account of the current state of affairs in Western societies.

The panopticon is a convenient starting point and a useful spatial metaphor to employ in teasing out a similar paradox in the critique of eth-nological representation. But there is also an important difference between the two cases. Foucault can insist that his knowledge of the panopticon is not imaginary but real as long as he does not claim that this form of power is all-encompassing and inescapable. For he apparently has been able to escape it.[5] Heterodox ethnographers, by contrast, cannot escape the logical paradox that plagues their discourse because they posit an epistemological rule that allows no exceptions. Yet the very positing of the rule is at the same time the exception that the rule excludes, so that the entire argument contradicts itself as soon as it is uttered. For if indeed it is the case, as heterodox ethnographers claim, that we are all caught within the circumstances of life and the circumstances of discourse, in short, within society and history, the question arises as to how they can be aware of this fact. How can they speak about these boundaries from a position within them? Is it not the case that to be aware of any sort of boundary and of the space it encloses as an *enclosed* space, one must have a view of the whole – a panoptic vision? And is it not true also that the only way to have access to such a view is from a position outside the boundary in question? The only way that one can know the forest as a forest rather than as so many trees is by stepping outside it, by putting a certain distance between oneself and the trees. And the reverse: one is in danger of losing sight of the forest by getting too close to the trees.

But beyond this metaphor, the paradox repeats itself at what one might call the epistemological level. To say that we are all caught within society and history is to argue that all knowledge is socially and historically determined. Yet it should be obvious that this epistemological argument already presupposes an inaugural cognitive act that is not subject to social and historical determination. Had this not been the case, no being living in society and history would ever be able to conceptualise this argument, no one would ever know that knowledge is in fact subject to social and historical conditions and conditionings. Since heterodox ethnographers are, by their own admission, socio-historical beings, we must assume, and they above all must recognise, that the epistemological argument may be applicable to all statements except the inaugural statement that makes it possible.

The epistemological argument, then, presupposes a certain definition of social reality that acts as its condition of possibility. This definition cannot be subject to the epistemological rule. It is a meta-epistemology, an ontology that sets up a domain of social reality in which the rule can operate. Without such an ontology, the epistemological argument is contradictory and self-defeating – it claims to know what, by its own admission, is impossible to know. Heterodox ethnographers pretend to be operating without the support of such an ontology. They pretend that their argument can stand on epistemological grounds alone. Hence, they cannot explain how socio-historical beings, such as themselves, can ever know anything at all about the socio-historical determination of knowledge.

The paradox that heterodox discourse runs into may be phrased in yet another way. If indeed it is humanly impossible to know how Others are in-themselves, does it make any sense to say that what ethnographers *can* know about them is 'fiction'? One would have thought that precisely because they can only know by means of their representations, what they do know is what actually exists – reality. Is this not, for instance, what we say about things that exist in space and time and reserve the term 'fiction' for things that we imagine to lie outside these cognitive boundaries? Indeed, the issue was settled, in the West at least, by Kant in the eighteenth century. In his attempt to curb what he perceived as the excesses of traditional (Christian) metaphysics, Kant demarcated the cognitive limits beyond which human thought should not venture. It is true that to do so, he was forced to posit another metaphysical realm – a reality in-itself – and hence he himself run into the same paradox that plagues heterodox discourse. For if by Kant's definition we can never know anything that lies outside time and space, how can he know that there is such a thing as a reality in-itself? Nonetheless, for Kant fiction and illusion were precisely all those statements that claimed to know the truth of this non-phenomenal reality – his inaugural positing of a reality in-itself excluded – not the statements about reality as it appears to us. Heterodox ethnographers turn Kant on his head. They argue that fiction is phenomenal reality – the way in which Others appear to ethnographers.

And yet, to say that something is 'fiction' already presupposes that one also knows what is not fiction, namely, the truth. Without the truth to act as a yardstick, heterodox ethnographers would have no reason to doubt the validity of ethnological knowledge. They would go about their ethnographic business without ever suspecting that the knowledge they and other ethnographers produce may be false. If they do doubt the validity of ethnological knowledge, it can only be because they know the truth about Others; they use it as a standard to measure the validity of ethnological knowledge and find that it falls short of this truth.

It would seem, then, that even though heterodox ethnographers are caught within society and history like everyone else, they are somehow able to step outside these boundaries and look at them from the outside; that some knowledge escapes social and historical determination; that heterodox ethnographers, if not anyone else, have managed, somehow, to gain access to the truth about Others, the deficient nature of all ethnological representations not withstanding. If we could, for the sake of argument, acknowledge this as a possibility, heterodox ethnographers must posit it as an indisputable fact. They must do so because this is the only way in which they can escape the paradox that plagues their discourse. But if they must recognise that they know the truth about Others, they can no longer maintain that there is a crisis in ethnological representation. They could certainly argue, as countless ethnographers have done and are doing, that certain representations are false, but they can no longer find fault with ethnological representation writ large.

There is, then, no epistemological problem in anthropology. Nor is it in fact the case that it is only heterodox ethnographers who know the truth about Others – all ethnographers do. This truth is what makes anthropology (and anthropologists) possible. It is the discipline's rationale and most fundamental representation.

Whether one can legitimately claim 'uncertainty about adequate means of describing social reality' in other human sciences (Marcus and Fischer 1986: 8) is debatable. In anthropology, however, there can hardly be any doubt about that domain of social reality occupied by Others. Far from being uncertain, ethnographers know *exactly* how Others are in-themselves – they are the Same as 'us'. For is it not the case that ethnographers, perhaps more than anyone else, struggle against racism and ethnocentrism? And is it not true also that they make this struggle one of their highest priorities? Do they not argue that racism is a mere fabrication with no foundation in reality whatsoever? And do they not also consider ethnocentrism a manifestation of Western cultural arrogance and ignorance combined? Do they not, in short, posit that Others are neither biologically nor culturally inferior to them? But if they do so, it is precisely because they already know that Others are in fact the Same.

But beyond the level of consciously positing Sameness in the struggle against racism and ethnocentrism, even if by default this notion is the structural condition of possibility of all statements that anthropology has ever produced about Others – whether statements about their kinship systems, magic and religion, politics, exchange or any other domain of ethnological investigation. To say this is not to claim that the way in which Sameness has been conceptualised and employed over the years and across paradigms has remained unchanged. Rather, it is to argue that whatever its particular historical manifestation, whatever the form it has assumed at different historical conjunctures and in different paradigms, Sameness understood as human unity has always been the ethnological a priori. It has been the axiomatic proposition that demarcated the epistemological space within which it became possible to study Others. Psychological Sameness – the 'psychic unity of mankind', as E.B. Tylor (1874) would have it – is the tenet made possible the study of Others, even if from a distance, as human rather than 'natural' beings, that is, as beings with social and cultural institutions. And in the twentieth century, cultural relativism, broadly understood, made fieldwork possible, since Other ways of life were now conceptualised, not as inferior manifestations of the European way of life but as cultures that embody the Same value and worth. This distinction does in fact point to the two broad and interrelated conceptions of Sameness as they emerge in the history of the discipline itself.

The beginning of anthropology as an academic discipline in the English-speaking world is usually associated with the appointment of Edward B. Tylor in 1884 as Reader at Oxford University. As Kuklick (1991) points out, before this time, the British Association for the Advancement of Science did not consider anthropology an independent domain of study and would not assign it its own section. What is perhaps more significant for the purposes of this discussion is that the Association classified anthropology under Natural History with such disciplines as 'geology, botany, zoology, and geography' (1981: 6). No doubt, beginnings are always arbitrary, but the change in anthropology's status and its subsequent development are not mere surface events. Nor can they be attributed solely or even mainly to the optimism about the potential of science that was prevalent at the time, as Kuklick seems to suggest. The change presupposes a radical shift at the ontological level, in the definition, that is, of the nature of human reality and, by extension, in Western perceptions of Others and Otherness. As long as Others were considered to be less than human, as they clearly were once visions of 'the natural man' and 'the noble savage' had lost their appeal to the European imagination,[6] anthropology or, better still, comparative ethnology could not have emerged and developed as it did. Racism, or what was at the time its biblical equivalent – polygenesis or the theory of multiple creations – kept anthropology chained to natural history; and it made the discipline appear to the learned of the time logically related to, and hence classifiable with such domains of knowledge as zoology and botany. Under such circumstances, Others could certainly be studied as part of nature and its history – as a natural resource perhaps, like animals and plants – but not as beings with social and cultural institutions, however 'primitive' and inferior.

Beyond optimism and the belief in the future of science, then, what was an even more fundamental requirement for the development of anthropology was a definition of humanity that did not exclude Others. For Edward Tylor, the paradigmatic figure of Victorian anthropology, this definition was none other than 'the psychic unity of mankind', the naturalist tenet first developed in the eighteenth century that posited the Same mental constitution for all peoples and at all times. It was this tenet that detached anthropology from nature and its history and transformed it into a social science.

No doubt, this universalistic claim raised thorny problems that scholars like Tylor had to grapple with. In particular, it was necessary to explain how the same mental constitution could give rise to such radically different ways of life; how, for example, rational human beings could entertain what Europeans perceived to be apparently irrational beliefs – magic being the paradigmatic case. And yet even raising such a question was already a step towards integrating Others into humanity, since however 'irrational' magical beliefs and practices may have been from the European point of view, they were clearly a human institution. One of Tylor's priorities, in fact, was to show that natives did engage in 'irrational' magico-religious practices, since the imputed lack of any sort of 'spiritual life' among natives was taken as proof of their sub-human condition. As one commentator put it, natives had 'nothing whatever of the character of religion, or of religious observance, to distinguish them from the beasts that perish'.[7] The existence of such blindness should come to us as no surprise. If one set out with the assumption that Others were, if not exactly 'beasts that perish', certainly less than human, one would not be looking for signs of spiritual life. Nor would one necessarily recognise them as such even when one came across them. As Tylor (1874: 418–19) pointed out, many of the writers who confidently declared the absence of magico-religious practices among native populations provided in the very same book evidence to the contrary. The possibility of perceiving native spiritual life, then, or any other native social institution and practice for that matter, presupposed a prior and more fundamental recognition – that Others were the Same kind of beings as Europeans, that is, human beings. Sameness at the psychological plane was the fundamental representation that made Victorian anthropology possible.

Having said that, Victorian anthropology could not have been anything other than the study of the origins and evolution of civilisation because it posited European culture as the pinnacle of human achievement. It could not have treated native populations as anything other than surviving specimens of the European past because, even though the paradigm acknowledged their humanity, it regarded their way of life as essentially inferior. Indeed, the notion that Others represent contemporary manifestations of different ways of life, so many versions of the Same fundamental experiment in social being, must have been inconceivable to Victorian anthropologists. Certainly, they would have not been able to appreciate Malinowski's (1922: 25) dictum, put forward half a century later, that the aim of anthropology should be 'to grasp the native's point of view, his relation to life, to realise *his* vision of *his* world'. Why should one want to understand the native's point of view when that view was fundamentally flawed? Why, for instance, should one bother to understand magic on its own terms when, as Tylor (1874: 112) confidently declared, it was 'one of the most pernicious delusions that ever vexed mankind'? Why bother, indeed, when one was already in possession of the most dependable means for gaining access to the truth of the physical world, namely, natural science?

The transformation of Victorian anthropology into what ethnographers recognise today as social and cultural anthropology became possible by means of another radical ontological shift in the meaning of human being. As is well known, this shift involved the relativisation of the notion of civilisation or, what is another way of saying the same thing, the pluralisation of the notion of culture. Beginning with Boas, culture is no longer understood in the singular, as something that societies have to a lesser or greater extent. Nor is it any longer understood as something on the basis of which societies can be placed in a hierarchy of value.[8] Rather, each society is now said to have *a* culture, its own unique way of organising life, which is no better and no worse than other ways of life. The causes of this transformation in ethnological sensibilities are complex and cannot be located solely within anthropology. If anything, they appear to be closely linked to a much wider aesthetic, intellectual and political movement – Romanticism – and the latter's revolt against the universalism of the Enlightenment. Indeed, as Lovejoy 1936: 239) points out, the most fundamental tenet of the Romantic movement was the idea that not only are there 'diverse excellences' in different ways of life 'but that diversity itself is of the essence of excellence'.

At the turn of the century, then, the idea that there are universal standards by which to measure the value of different ways of life and that Europe itself is the standard to do so is beginning to lose credibility. Psychological Sameness is no longer expected to produce the same culture across the board. On the contrary, common humanity is now located in cultural diversity, since to be human now means to be different and unique.

Paradoxically, being different now becomes the surest sign of being the Same, difference at the level of cultural form becomes Sameness at the level of cultural value. It was this new definition of human reality – cultural diversity as 'diverse excellences' – that made it possible for Malinowski to posit 'the native's point of view' as the fundamental goal of ethnological understanding. It was this postulate that made his argument not only thinkable and utterable but also reproducible as a serious statement. For if the 'native's point of view' was significant in its own right, if it carried as much weight as any other point of view, it was a legitimate object of scientific investigation. Indeed, Malinowski (1922: 25) hoped that, by grasping how Others lived, 'man's mentality will be revealed to us ... along some lines which we never have followed before'. He hoped that, by understanding 'human nature in a shape very distant and foreign to us, we shall have some light shed on our own'.

There was much to be learned from natives, then, and of the greatest importance. Hence the need for not just any kind of investigation of native life, but for a committed, methodical and extended scrutiny of it from the closest possible range. And hence Malinowski's insistence that it was time for anthropologists to become ethnographers, to leave their armchairs and speculations behind, to 'get off the veranda' and pitch their tents among the natives. Fieldwork, and all twentieth-century ethnological paradigms that have embraced and made it their condition of possibility, presuppose the fundamental recognition that Other cultures are as significant as the cultures of the West, that in them one can discern, in a different form no doubt, the Same content – 'man's mentality' – what it means to be human. In short, the new method of acquiring knowledge about Others presupposes a new social ontology – Sameness at the level of cultural value and worth.

Contrary to all appearances, then, the heterodox critique and the consensus that it has generated in the discipline notwithstanding, there is no epistemological problem in anthropology; or, to be more precise, if there is a problem, it cannot be epistemological. Ethnographers do know the truth about Others; not only do they know it, but they also strive to demonstrate it in practice. Indeed, as I will try to show in the next chapter, the history of the discipline is in a fundamental sense the history of the ethnographer's struggle to uphold Sameness in the face of representations of Otherness that contradict and undermine it.

And yet clearly there is a problem with anthropology which is not merely an ethnological problem but also a problem for those at the receiving end of the discipline – its objects of study and subjects of its power. The history of the discipline may be a record of the ethnographer's struggle to demonstrate Sameness and to redeem Others but it also stands witness to the monumental failure to do so. There is no ethnological paradigm – be it evolutionism, functionalism, structuralism or culturalism – that has not been found guilty, to a lesser or greater extent, for one reason or another of the ultimate ethnological transgression – ethnocentrism.[9] There is no paradigm that has not reproduced further down the road the very divisions of the world that, ironically, it sets out to eradicate. Ethnographers may or may not get used to the 'burden of authorship', but should anyone expect natives to get used to the burden of Otherness that ethnographers impose on them?

The ethnological problem and the problem of Otherness are inextricably intertwined. In the aftermath of the heterodox critique, ethnographers have come to view the former in epistemological terms and the latter as a question that could be resolved if only the problem of knowledge can be somehow bypassed. But the ethnological problem is surely not epistemological and the problem of Otherness cannot be explained in terms of the limits of ethnological knowledge. The discipline posits the unity of the world axiomatically – a priori – but is unable to demonstrate what it posits and is itself implicated in what it strives to refute. It is this that constitutes the ethnological problem and not, as heterodox discourse claims, the presumed inability to know the truth about Others. What needs to be explained is how ethnographers, armed as they are with the truth about their object of study – namely, that Others are essentially and fundamentally the Same as them – end up, despite themselves, reproducing an image of the world in which Others emerge as their inferiors.

3   THE SALVATION INTENT

THE THREE STRATEGIES OF REDEMPTION

From its early stirrings in the writings of the Spanish missionaries and theologians in the sixteenth century to its inception as an academic discipline in the nineteenth to the present day, ethnological thought and practice have been deeply marked by a salvation intent. This intent is not to be confused with the early twentieth-century preoccupation with disappearing Others and the concomitant attempts to preserve their way of life in written memory – to preserve them, that is, for scientific perusal as so many monuments of experimentation 'with the possibilities of the human spirit' (Mead 1930: 10). Nor is it to be confused with the more recent and related fear about what is perceived as an irrevocable trend towards global homogenisation and Westernisation, encapsulated, for instance, in Lévi-Strauss's (1973: 44) famous lamentation that 'mankind has opted for monoculture'. These preoccupations, whether for the good of science or for the good of humanity, are a consequence of a much more fundamental and enduring aim – one, moreover, that is both logically and historically prior to the concern with preservation. This aim is none other than the redemption of Otherness in the eyes of its Western observers and critics. Anthropology takes it upon itself to save Others from the calumny of inferiority – whatever this presumed inferiority's historical manifestations – by striving to demonstrate that they are ultimately and essentially the Same as the self.

In the wake of the heterodox critique of ethnographic authority – the authority to define Others – it is easy to lose sight of this fundamental ethnological intent. Anthropology does not so much seek to define Others as to *redefine* them in order to redeem them. It does not so much seek to discover the truth about them as to demonstrate what it already knows and posits as the truth. This distinction is significant because it raises important questions about anthropology in general and heterodox discourse in particular. The latter, being consistent with the argument that ethnological representations are mediated by power and rhetoric, does not attempt to represent Others. Rather, it makes ethnological discourse and practice themselves its object of study; and because it does not talk about 'them' but about 'us', it provides a testing ground for its own epistemological claims. If heterodox discourse can avoid the ethnocentric pitfalls of earlier ethnological paradigms, then we can be fairly certain that it is because of their Westernness – their geopolitical position and cultural identity – that ethnographers divide the world.

The ethnological salvation intent manifests itself in three analytically distinct but in practice interrelated strategies of redemption. The first strategy locates manifestations of the Self in Other societies in an effort to mediate the opposition and to show that Others are far more similar to the West than it may at first appear. In the history of the Western colonisation of the rest of the world, Others were often found to be lacking certain 'fundamental' institutions – institutions, that is, taken to be exemplary of the Western self and hence posited as the very hallmark of humanity. Typically, and depending on what was considered to be fundamental at different historical periods, Others were shown to be deprived of religion, family, government and, more recently, self-regulating market structures. A more persistent and diachronic theme refers to the Others' lack of 'practical rationality', that is, ultimately to an imputed inability to distinguish between the empirical and metaphysical worlds.

The ethnological response to all such allegations has always been the same, namely, to locate the very institutions and forms of rationality of which Others' societies were allegedly deprived in the midst of native life. The problem, according to the ethnological argument, is not that Others have no religion, family or government or that they are incapable of coming to terms with the realities of the empirical world. Rather, it is that Western observers themselves misinterpret native lives and overlook the existence of these institutions and practices. No doubt, social institutions like religion and family often take different forms from those in the West, while practical rationality may be less central in some societies than in others. But it is one thing to point this out and quite another to say that they do not exist at all. What is required to locate such institutions in native societies is readiness to unburden oneself of excessive cultural baggage, willingness to set aside Western presumptions of cultural superiority and to take a closer look.

This strategy is well illustrated in the recent debate between Obeyesekere (1992) and Sahlins (1985, 1995) about Captain Cook's encounter with the natives of Hawaii. The controversy is about how natives think and, as will become apparent below, it resurrects the very ghosts that Evans-Pritchard put to rest in the 1930s, having won a similar debate with Lévy-Bruhl. For Sahlins (1985: xii), who follows both Lévy-Bruhl and Lévi-Strauss, societies 'are differentially "open" to history', which means that some are more prone to historical change than others. The difference has to do with the distance between a society's symbolic system and the empirical world. The less abstract and metaphysical the symbolic system, the more likely it is to be contradicted by empirical reality. The categories of the symbolic system are then revised to overcome the contradiction and this in turn leads to social change. The Hawaiian symbolic system of the eighteenth century, Sahlins argues, appears to have been fairly non-empirical. Hence, when Captain Cook landed at Hawaii and the local inhabitants mistook him for one of the local deities, there was little that could happen by way of contradiction to change the natives' mind. Indeed, it was this misconception, according to Sahlins, that ultimately led to Captain Cook's death.[1]

In his response, as in countless other similar efforts to locate manifestations of the self in Other societies, Obeyesekere proceeds deductively from the a priori postulate of Sameness. As he points out, '"practical rationality" ... *must* exist in most, if not all, societies, admittedly in varying degrees of importance' (1992: 205, n. 48; my emphasis). Indeed, Obeyesekere (1992: 19) argues, echoing a similar claim made by Evans-Pritchard in the 1930s, 'it is hard to imagine how people could conduct their economic lives without such "practical rationality"'. Take, for instance, 'the extraordinary [sic] complex system of fish ponds ... that the Hawaiians developed'. Such a system 'could not have functioned without managerial skills and practical rationality' (1992: 205, n. 49). But if the Hawaiians could deal so well with the empirical world, it is highly unlikely that they would mistake Captain Cook for a god. Rather, Obeyesekere goes on to argue, Sahlins's claim suggests that, ironically, it is the Western imagination itself that has difficulties coming to terms with empirical reality or, at any rate, with the empirical reality of colonial encounters. Claims such as Sahlins's perpetuate the myth that the colonised deified their European colonisers.

The second strategy of redemption is essentially a reversal of the first. Its aim is to locate manifestations of Otherness in Western societies and in this way demonstrate that 'we' are not so radically different from 'them', as models of binary oppositions often suggest. Ethnographers, according to the argument, are as likely to overlook traits of Otherness in their own societies as anyone else. Since their primary concern is the study of Others, they often take on board uncritically abstract models of their own societies developed by other disciplines and use these models as if they were reality. This, coupled with the theoretical models that ethnographers develop about Other societies, produce an image of the world in which the two admittedly different sociocultural universes – West and Other – appear to have nothing at all in common.

The aim of this strategy is to underscore the similarities by showing that the West has its own share of Otherness. In particular, ethnographers seek to locate in the West what is taken to be the most fundamental characteristic of Otherness, namely, a certain irrationalism that, for example, manifests itself in mystical beliefs and practices. I shall explore in detail several ethnological attempts to locate the 'irrational' Other in the West in the next two sections. For now, I wish to turn briefly to a recent example of how ethnographers discover Otherness within – the Otherness of gift exchange. I should point out that, in this example, the gift has little to do with the positive image that Mauss constructed in his classic treatment of the topic. Rather it refers to gift exchange as it appears from a far more rationalistic and economistic perspective.[2]

As is well known, Mauss celebrates gift relations because he valorises the moral system on which they are based. This moral system, according to Mauss (1967 [1925]: 66), is an expression of 'the purer sentiments', namely, 'charity, social service and solidarity'. As such, gift exchange is something to be emulated. The same kind of sympathetic treatment is found in many other, subsequent ethnographic writings, particularly of those who are critical of Western capitalism and its commodity relations.[3] But this treatment hardly exhausts what has been said about the gift. In the West, gift exchange has long been associated with traditionalism and backwardness, while in its more accentuated form, such as the potlatch, it appears as a heedless and needless squandering of resources – a practice motivated by irrational impulses. In the same vein, and from a rather different perspective, gift relations appear as a sort of underground, underdeveloped and inferior market structure. The difference hinges on the distinction between a market 'in itself' and a market 'for itself', as Bourdieu (1977) would have it, that is, a market oblivious to its own existence and function and one that, having been objectified, is fully aware of itself. In effect, it is a difference between those who are at the mercy of blind societal forces and those who have mastered and brought them under their control. It is this image that motivates ethnological attempts to locate gift relations in Western societies – an image of Otherness – not the kind depicted by Mauss and other sympathetic scholars.

In a recent article entitled 'Occidentalism', as well as in subsequent work – all of which has been inspired by Said's *Orientalism* – Carrier (1992, 1995) sets out to demarcate the various gift domains in an otherwise commodity-dominated capitalist landscape.[4] Gift relations, Carrier points out, were very much part of retail trade well into the twentieth century, albeit this no longer appears to be the case. And they are still the dominant paradigm in the context of interpersonal relations, particularly the family, as well as at the fringes of the capitalist economy, such as the black market. For Carrier this demonstrates that, although West and Other are different in this respect, the difference has been exaggerated. The Otherness of gift exchange is firmly rooted in the West.

Carrier's attempt to locate the Other in the West is not without problems. As I have argued elsewhere (Argyrou 1996a), the argument is haunted by the spectre of evolutionism, since it cannot avoid the implication that gift relations survive in the West from an earlier, less rationalised era. Nor does the argument have the effect that Carrier intended. One could point out, for example, that if gift relations were very much in evidence in retail trade well into the twentieth century and no longer are, this is surely an indication that this form of Otherness is disappearing. Much the same case can be made about the claim that the gift is still the dominant paradigm in interpersonal relations. Western claims that gift exchange is motivated by irrational impulses are not meant to apply to all manifestations of the gift, only to those areas of public life, such as the market, which are *expected* to be rationalised.

The two strategies of redemption discussed so far are rather modest in their scope. Their aim is not so much to negate difference as to demonstrate that it is unduly exaggerated, that in reality 'we' and 'they' have a great deal in common. What they do not do is to deal with Otherness itself, which remains to be explained and continues to haunt the ethnological imagination. It is this undoubtedly much more complex and difficult problem that the third strategy of redemption undertakes to tackle. This strategy goes beyond empirical phenomena – locating this or that institution or practice in this or that society – and strives to demonstrate the truth of the unseen. Its aim is to show that the world is united by something far more fundamental than mere similarity, something that obliterates all distance between Self and Other and binds the world into the unity of the Same. In short, this strategy strives to demonstrate identity. In its broadest outline, the third strategy of redemption consists of a radical reinterpretation of Otherness, a magical act of purification in its own right. It is an attempt to show that even though difference has form, it lacks any real content or, what is another way of saying that same thing, that the content of Otherness is the Same, despite its obviously different form.

Historically, the third strategy of redemption proceeds from two different points of departure. In the ethnological thought of the sixteenth century and in the writings of Victorian anthropology, the point of departure was an all-embracing universalism. In the former case this universalism was based on biblical postulates, in the latter on naturalist ones, but in both (the Same) human nature was required to double itself at the level of culture and produce the Same sort of civilisation across the board or, at least, a Sameness that lay within a recognisable range of difference. The ethnological problem to be resolved, then, was how human nature could give rise to something Other than itself, as it apparently did in the form of cultures that were radically different from what Europeans considered to be the only possible one – their own. The answer to this question, and the metaphor used to render this answer plausible, was in both cases the same: Otherness is an incomplete manifestation of the Same, a stage in its natural unfolding towards full realisation; it is very much like childhood, itself only a stage in the natural evolution towards the maturity of adulthood. To be sure, this natural process of cultural development was in the case of the Other arrested by historical contingencies, perhaps even unfavourable environmental conditions. Nonetheless, the argument continued, once such obstacles were removed, the content of Otherness – which is the Same – would blossom into its full and predetermined form. At this point, difference would cease to exist as such and Other societies would no longer be distinguishable as Other; they would not only be, but also look the Same.

As I have suggested in the last chapter, at the turn of the century, the notion that Others were an incomplete and hence inferior manifestation of the self was increasingly becoming unacceptable to ethnographers. This change in ethnological sensibilities was to transform the nature of the ethnological problem itself and the way in which ethnographers sought to resolve it. The point of departure of the ethnological endeavour was no longer psychological Sameness, since this was by now taken for granted in the discipline. Rather, it was Sameness at the level of cultural value and worth, the notion that, despite differences, Other societies embody the Same cultural value as Western societies. The ethnological problem was no longer how to show that what was culturally inferior could eventually become the Same, but rather that difference was in fact already the Same, that what appeared to be culturally inferior was in reality only culturally different – simply another way of doing the very Same thing. There have been numerous conceptualisations in the discipline as to what the 'Same thing' is, but here I shall refer briefly and rather schematically only to the most important of these notions.

Early in the twentieth century, ethnological thought was guided by the notion that social and cultural institutions exist because they meet the needs of individuals – their psychological as well as social needs. Round about the same time, the paradigm inspired by Durkheimian sociology brought to the forefront the needs of society, essentially stability and reproduction. Subsequent paradigms focused on the need to classify the things of the world, to create conceptual order out of chaos, while in another transmutation of this theme, the emphasis was placed on the need for meaning, whether semantic, existential or both. In each of these cases the strategy of redemption that ethnographers adopted was always the same: pick a trait of Otherness, place it within the wider context of the society in question and demonstrate that, within this context, it fulfils the Same universal human need. Magico-religious systems, for example, in many ways the paradigmatic manifestation of Otherness, have been shown to soothe anxiety and fear (Malinowski), to reproduce the bonds of solidarity (Radcliffe-Brown, Evans-Pritchard), to establish conceptual order in the natural and social worlds (Lévi-Strauss, Mary Douglas), to explain misfortune and other inexplicable events and hence to maintain faith in the ultimate meaningfulness and purposefulness of the world (Evans-Pritchard, Geertz). It was in this perhaps inescapably functionalist mode of reasoning that Otherness was tackled by twentieth-century anthropology, in this way that it was made to yield what ethnographers have always known it to embody – Sameness in terms of cultural value. Through interpretation, which is to say, purification, Otherness emerged as a reasonable way of dealing with universal human predicaments, a different way no doubt, but an understandable one nonetheless.

In a text intended for the non-specialist, Peter Metcalf (1978: 6) outlines clearly and concisely this strategy of redemption at a general enough level to encompass all the major twentieth-century ethnological paradigms:

First, we seek the exotic. ... Second, we try to fit this alien item – cultural trait, custom, piece of behavior – into its social and cultural context, thereby reducing it to a logical, sensible, even necessary element. Having done that, we feel that we can understand why people do, or say, or think something instead of being divorced from them by what they say, think or do.

The greatest reservation, then, that which keeps 'us' at a distance from 'them', appears to be the misconception that Others do what they do (or think, or say) for no apparent reason, that is, in effect, that they behave irrationally. If ethnographers can show that there are 'logical' and 'sensible' grounds for their behaviour, if they can make people see the sense and value in what Others do, the gap that divides the world begins to close. For people now see in Others what they would probably do, think or say under similar circumstances; they would begin to see in them their own selves.

There is hardly an ethnographer – this one included – who has not deployed one or more of these three redemptive strategies, hardly anyone who has not attempted to locate the West in the Other or the Other within or to demonstrate Otherness's very Same content. Moreover, all three strategies have been in currency for centuries, certainly well before anthropology became an academic discipline. The story of this deployment, then, is long and in a certain sense repetitive. But it must be told nonetheless, and in the greatest possible detail. For it stands witness to anthropology's monumental failure to demonstrate what it knows and posits axiomatically; and it brings to the fore the paradoxical fact that the discipline is itself implicated in the very reproduction of what it strives to refute. This story must be told not only because it reveals a terrible secret – that no matter how hard and how long they strive, ethnographers can never redeem Otherness – but also because it announces a more auspicious one – that Others do not need ethnographers to redeem them, that they can do so by themselves.

CHRISTIAN ETHNOLOGY AND VICTORIAN ANTHROPOLOGY

The first scholars to engage Otherness in an ethnological sense, that is, not simply as a curio but as something to be explained and ultimately redeemed, were the Spanish theologians and missionaries of the sixteenth century.[5] The popular, and scientific, image of the inhabitants of the New World circulating in Europe at the time was of a people unlike anything that Europeans had encountered before. American Indians were said to live in the wild, to wear no clothes and to have no social institutions, whether government, family or religion. They were said to engage in sexual intercourse publicly and indiscriminately, practise human sacrifice and some, like the Carib, were reputed to commit the penultimate horror – cannibalism. In short, this was an image of a people behaving in bizarre, aberrant and horrid ways, of a kind of life that, as far as Europeans were concerned, no rational human being would ever lead. Hence the inevitable and crucial question raised in some quarters: were American Indians endowed with reason at all? Indeed, were they fully human?

Many sixteenth-century Europeans responded to this question by invoking what is effectively the biblical version of racism. This doctrine, known as 'polygenesis', posited multiple Creations or, at any rate, an original Creation for Europeans and another, secondary one for American Indians. Other sceptics had recourse to the classical Greek notion of autochthony, the spontaneous emergence of people from the Earth, and argued that American Indians were perhaps such earthly creatures. In either case, the 'problem of recognition' (Pagden 1982: 10–14), the question of what exactly were the natives of the New World was for these Europeans effectively resolved. American Indians behaved in bizarre and aberrant ways precisely because they were not quite the same kind of beings as Europeans, that is, not fully human.

To the Spanish theologians and missionaries like Vitoria and Las Casas, theories of polygenesis and autochtony were nothing short of blasphemies. They contradicted blatantly one of the most fundamental tenets of the Christian canon – the belief that all beings originated in one Creation and that all humans were children of God and the Same in the eyes of God. This tenet of common humanity applied as much to Christians as to 'infidels', like the Turks, and 'pagans', like Africans. Being a universal principle, it had to apply to American Indians as well. The Spanish churchmen of the sixteenth century, then, were confronted with a formidable intellectual challenge, namely, to explain why American Indians behaved so much unlike human beings – the standard of humanity being the culture of sixteenth-century Europe. Their task was to find ways to redeem American Indian Otherness and to save the natives of the New World from de-humanisation.

The mistreatment and enslavement of American Indians by the Spanish conquerors and settlers alike, of which Las Casas (1992 [1542]) provides a vivid account, was rationalised on the basis of Aristotle's theory of natural slavery. According to this theory, human beings are distinguished from animals by the faculty of reason, but not all human beings are able to employ reason equally effectively. For Aristotle, slaves were human beings of the latter sort. Their intellect was not powerful enough to exercise effective control over the animalistic side of their nature, the passions and instincts. Thus, if they were to lead a human life at all, it was necessary to place such individuals under the control and guidance of a master. Something of a similar nature was postulated about American Indians as well. It was clear to the Europeans of the sixteenth century that American Indians were not in full control of their passions and instincts. It was equally clear to them, however, that they were not mere animals either. Rather, many concluded, American Indians constituted a third species of beings that, in the 'Great Chain of Being' (cf. Lovejoy 1936), occupied an intermediate position between beasts and humans. In his infinite wisdom, God created them to serve human beings, namely, the European colonisers, and in serving their masters to attain whatever level of humanity they were capable of ever attaining.

But what was the nature of human being? As Pagden shows, sixteenth-century thought was heavily influenced by Aristotelian ideas that posited the life of the city as the most fundamental characteristic of humanity. The city was not merely understood as a physical locality but also, more importantly, as a domain of organised social life. It was only in the city and by means of structured and regulated social relations that human beings could attain the goal of life, namely, virtue and happiness. With this tenet in mind, and in what must be one of the earliest ethnological works, the Spanish theologian Vitoria set out to defend American Indians by locating manifestations of this fundamental characteristic of humanity among the natives of the New World. The evidence was overwhelming and incontrovertible. As Pagden (1982: 71) points out, the great cities of the Mexica and the Inca had always been an object of European attention: 'Cortés compared [them] to Seville and Cordoba, Toribio de Montolinia to Jerusalem and Babylon, and Garcilaso de la Vega to Rome.' People who were capable of constructing and operating cities of such enormous complexity, Vitoria argued, could hardly be deficient in their rational faculties.

Another important trait of civility and humanity on Vitoria's list was religion. As I have already suggested, American Indians, as well as Other natives, were often reputed to have no religion at all – an argument that had as much currency in Victorian England as in sixteenth-century Europe. Once again, the Indians of central and south America served as an exemplary model.

The Mexica and the Inca had all the things that Christians understood by the word 'church': a cult, places of worship and a priesthood – an organization, that is, which was empowered to mediate between man and God and which played a directive role in the life of the community. ... All of these things were proof that, although Indians may have wandered very far from the truth, they knew at least what form the truth should take. (Pagden 1982: 78–9)

For Vitoria, then, and for other Spanish theologians and missionaries, although American Indians were apparently different from Europeans in many respects, they nonetheless exhibited fundamental characteristics of humanity. If one approached them without prejudice or a desire to exploit them, it was easy to discern in the midst of their Otherness unequivocal manifestations of the Self.

Three centuries later, the practice of locating manifestations of the Self in Other societies was to become one of the most important redemptive strategies of academic anthropology. But so was the reverse strategy that the Spanish churchmen first employed, namely, the practice of locating manifestations of Otherness in the West. In his confrontation with other Spanish scholars, Vitoria was quick to point out that Otherness was by no means the sad prerogative of American Indians. No doubt, the latter were different from many Europeans but not from all Europeans. Indeed, to Vitoria, they appeared to resemble in many ways the European lower classes. 'Even among our own people', Vitoria argued, 'we can see many peasants who are little different from brute animals'. As Pagden points out, Vitoria's analogy:

was an obvious and instructive one. To all educated town-dwelling men the [European] peasantry seemed close in condition, if not in kind, to the animals among which they worked. Like Indians, they were deprived of any real understanding of the world around them. ... The European peasantry ... had no obvious share in the civil life and were thought to be still less capable of what one observer called 'the superior exercises of the soul'. (1982: 97)

Vitoria's comparison between European peasants and American Indians 'was echoed by nearly everyone who came into contact with [the latter]', according to Pagden (1982: 98) – by nearly everyone, one might add, whose goal was to save American Indians from de-humanisation.

In an interesting twist of the same theme – the practice, that is, of locating Otherness within – the Spanish missionary Las Casas did not hesitate to apply Vitoria's description of European peasants as 'brute animals' to Europeans of a higher standing. Las Casas travelled to the New World and was appalled by the savagery and ferocity that the *conquistadores* and Spanish settlers exhibited toward American Indians. The Spaniards, he points out in a characteristic passage of his treatise, became so 'anaesthetized to human suffering by their own greed and ambition that they ceased to be men in any meaningful sense' (1992 [1542]: 3); they 'fell like ravening wolves upon the [natives], or like tigers and savage lions who have not eaten meat for days' (1992: 11). It is significant to note that in these quotations Las Casas reverses symbolically accusations of cannibalism, and by doing so demonstrates that savagery, the alleged prerogative of Others, has deep roots even in the most cultivated soil.

Although quite useful in undermining radical distinctions between Europeans and American Indians, there was so much that this particular strategy could achieve. Indeed, pushed to its logical extreme, the argument that animality could also be located within European societies would de-humanise both those sections of the European population to which it was applied and American Indians as well. It would, in other words, defeat the purpose of the exercise, which was none other than upholding the divine principle of common humanity. To avoid this pitfall, it was necessary for the Spanish churchmen to grapple with Otherness itself and to explain why human beings appeared to behave like 'animals'. In this task, they had recourse to what ethnographers today would call a metaphor of mediation, a term that would bridge the gap between 'animalistic' and human behaviour in such a way as to make possible the transition from the former to the latter. The metaphor used was that of children. Rather than being a third species between beasts and human beings, American Indians, the Spanish churchmen pointed out, were 'some variety of fully grown child[ren] whose rational faculties were complete but still more potential than actual' (Pagden 1982: 104). Like children, they were 'unreflective, passion dominated, half-reasoning being[s]' (1982: 105), but unlike beings of another species, American Indians could gradually develop and reach the level of European civility and culture. What they required to achieve this level of development was not mistreatment and enslavement but, as in the case of children, education and guidance.

The critical children metaphor, then, made it possible for the Spanish churchmen to argue that American Indians were well within the parameters of the Same. On the basis of this metaphor they were able to claim that, despite its obviously different form, American Indian Otherness had the Same content as European civilisation. Rather than being a different nature and hence an irrevocable condition, American Indian Otherness was a different history of the Same nature. It was a history that, for whatever reason, arrested development and prevented human nature from following its pre-determined course. As a history, however, it was amenable to change and reform. It was redeemable.

There is an important theme in this sixteenth-century story that requires further comment. It is the context in which the salvation intent emerges and becomes such a crucial element in the lives of men like Vitoria and Las Casas. As I have already suggested, this context was delimited by the Spanish churchmen's uncompromising belief in the tenet of common humanity, itself the outcome of faith in a divinely determined order. The story, then, posits an important link between Otherness and the salvation intent, namely, religion. If one is prepared to treat religion the way in which the dominant ethnological paradigms do, that is, as a transcendental symbol that transforms the being here and now into significant being, the link may prove far more important that it might first appear. Here it should suffice to say that in this context, Sameness begins to emerge as a transcendental symbol in its own right and the discipline's salvation intent as an attempt by the ethnographer to maintain an ethically meaningful vision of the world that Otherness, left to its own devices, threatens to destroy. I shall return to this issue and explore it in detail in Chapter 5. I now turn to Victorian anthro-pology and its own deployment of the same three strategies of redemption.

Almost three centuries after the work of Vitoria and Las Casas, anthro-pology, now a recognised academic discipline, would return to children as the primary metaphor of mediation between Self and Others. This is partic-ularly evident in the work of E.B. Tylor, the paradigmatic figure, perhaps, of Victorian anthropology. Tylor was writing at a time that was quite receptive to racist ideas, whether in the form of polygenetic theories or of racial inter-pretations of Darwin's theory of evolution. As Stocking (1987: 159) points out, racism offended Tylor's 'humanitarian Quaker principles';[6] it also ran counter to the tenets of the naturalist, rationalist ideology that he whole-heartedly espoused. The most fundamental of these tenets were the twin notions of the universality and regularity of the laws of nature. The former was guaranteed by the Creator of the world, the latter by the fact that God chose to manifest himself through natural law rather than by erratically suspending it, as in earlier times when miracles were still possible.[7] Since human beings were part of nature, their minds, and therefore their behaviour, were themselves governed by immutable laws – the laws of human nature. 'It is no more reasonable to suppose the laws of mind differently constituted in Australia and in England, in the time of cave-dwellers and in the time of the builders of sheet-iron houses', Tylor (1874: 158–9) argued in a well-known passage, 'than to suppose that the laws of chemical combination were of one sort in the time of coal-measures, and are of another now'.

The 'laws of mind', being natural laws, applied to all peoples at all times and constituted what Tylor called 'the psychic unity of mankind'. This unity, in turn, combined with the similarities in life's circumstances – itself the outcome of the universality of natural law – meant that human institutions were bound to be similar, both historically and cross-culturally. Given these premises, Tylor was eager to refute European claims that certain societies were so primitive as to lack basic human institutions. As I have already suggested, lack of religion was an especially popular claim. For instance, in his address to the Ethnological Society of London in 1866, the famous British explorer, Sir James Baker, had this to say about Nilotic peoples: 'Without any exception, they are without a belief in a supreme being, neither have they any form of worship or idolatry; nor is the darkness of their minds enlightened by even a ray of superstition.'[8] To be pagan or infidel was perhaps understandable; to lack any form of worship whatsoever, however, was a rather different matter. It raised serious doubts about one's humanity.

For Tylor, lack of anything so fundamental as religion in native societies was highly improbable. It was more likely that people like Sir James Baker used 'wide words in a narrow sense' (Tylor 1874: 419), that is, religion as it was understood and practised in European societies. As a result, Europeans end up attributing 'irreligion to tribes whose doctrines are unlike theirs in much the same manner as theologians have so often attributed atheism to tribes whose deities differed from their own' (1874: 420). If one defines religion in terms of a 'belief in a supreme deity or of judgement after death', Tylor (1874: 424) pointed out, many native societies would be found to be lacking religion. But such a definition would be mistaken because it identifies religion not with what is universal about it, but with one of its many historical manifestations. For his part, Tylor defined religion in the broadest possible sense – as belief in spiritual being. Hence, he was able to argue that there was hardly any native society without religion, nowhere that this fundamental human institution did not take root.

Yet, even if one was to accept Tylor's minimalist definition of religion and acknowledge its existence in native societies, what was one to make of magic – of witchcraft, haruspications, rhavdomancy, dactyliomancy, and other such bizarre-sounding and alien practices in which natives were known to engage? Were not these proof that natives were fundamentally different from

Europeans or, at any rate, evidence of their complete and utter irrationality? For Tylor, magic was indeed an illusion but it was an illusion that arose from a misunderstanding of the way in which the natural world operates rather than from any inherent inability to reason correctly. Moreover, magic was by no means the prerogative of natives. It was still very much part of life in European societies, particularly the life of the peasantry and the lower classes. The magical practices of the 'lower races',[9] Tylor (1874: 118) pointed out, 'are fully rivalled [by] superstitions which still hold their ground in Europe'. For example, 'the German cottager declares that if a dog howls looking downward, it portends a death'; the Hessian youth 'thinks that he may escape the conscription by carrying a baby-girl's cap in his pocket'; and the Cornishman says that fish 'should be eaten from the tail towards the head, to bring other fishes' heads towards the shore' (1874: 118–19). As for Protestants, who are supposed to be hostile to religious superstitions, 'they get the Catholic priests and monks to help them against witchcraft, to lay ghosts, consecrate herbs and discover thieves' (1874: 115).

It was clear to Tylor, then, that magic and other superstitious beliefs and practices persisted as survivals among the lower European classes. Nor was this all, in fact. As Tylor complains, there was actually a revival of this 'savage philosophy' among the higher classes in the form of spiritualism. There were 'tens of thousands' of spiritualists both in England and the United States, according to Tylor, and among them one could even find 'men of distinguished mental power' (1874: 142). Thus, even though overlooked by many, Tylor was able to show that the form of Otherness associated with magic, mysticism, spiritualism, in a word, irrationalism, was firmly rooted in Western societies themselves.

There were, then, many similarities between native and Western societies, many ways in which they resembled one another. Yet, when everything was said and done, Otherness itself, whether within or without, still remained an inexplicable and troublesome presence. And for as long as it remained inexplicable, the ground on which the universalistic claim of the 'psychic unity of mankind' rested was far from being secured. For if the 'laws of mind' that accounted for rational thinking and action were everywhere and at all times the same, how could they give rise to such 'irrationalities' as witchcraft and spiritualism? Either these beliefs and practices were not quite what they appeared to be or the tenet of the 'psychic unity of mankind' was fundamentally flawed. This was the rather vexing problem that confronted Tylor and other evolutionists. Luckily, the ground for resolving it had already been laid by the British empiricists of the eighteenth century, whose thinking Tylor followed quite closely.

To begin with, by 'laws of mind' Tylor meant the three principles of associating ideas, best exemplified perhaps in the work of David Hume. As is well known, for Hume (1977 [1748]: 11) all ideas originate in experience and are nothing more than 'copies of our impressions'. Nonetheless, the human mind has the ability to combine these 'copies' of reality and to produce an even greater number of ideas. There are three ways in which the mind associates ideas, according to Hume: by means of resemblance, contiguity in time and space and cause and effect. Thus, a picture may lead the mind to think of the original: the sight of one's house could give rise to thoughts of one's neighbours and a wound to thoughts of the pain that it causes.

To account for the Otherness of magic without compromising the tenet of the 'psychic unity of mankind', Tylor needed only to follow Hume and the latter's explanation of a similar 'irrationalism' – the Christian belief in miracles. 'The imagination of man', Hume (1977: 112) wrote:

is naturally sublime, delighted with whatever is remote and extraordinary, and running, without control, into the most distant parts of space and time in order to avoid the objects, which custom rendered too familiar to it. A correct *Judgement* observes a contrary method and ... confines itself to common life, and to such subjects that fall under daily practices and experience; leaving the more sublime topics to the embellishment of poets and orators, or the arts of priests and politicians.

The 'imagination', then, being by its very nature 'sublime' and rhetorical, lies outside the domain of 'correct judgement.' It may be useful for artistic purposes, but it is ill-suited for the serious world of science and practical activity. Under certain circumstances, it can lead people completely astray. This is particularly the case when 'gross and vulgar passions' are allowed free rein. In such cases 'correct judgement' is either completely abandoned or 'the regularity of its operations' is severely disrupted (1977: 79). As a result, people begin to mistake the product of their minds for reality. A case in point is miracles which, as Hume (1977: 76) points out, are 'a violation of the laws of nature'. Belief in 'real presence', for example, that is, belief in the presence of the body and blood of Christ in the bread and wine of the Eucharist, is precisely one of those instances were the 'picture' is confused with the 'original' and the symbol becomes what it represents. Because 'fancy or the affections' (1977: 79) are not kept under control, reason becomes clouded and can no longer distinguish between what the imagination conjures up and what is actually real.

Not surprisingly, in his exposition of magic, Tylor follows Hume to the letter. The 'occult sciences', he argued, are the product of the universal principles of the mind, 'the Association of Ideas'. However, Tylor (1874: 116) points out, even though this 'faculty ... lies at the very foundation of human reason', it can be the basis 'of human unreason also'. As in the case of Christian miracles, magic inverts the process of associating ideas and in effect makes mockery of reason.

Man, as yet in a low intellectual condition, having come to associate in thought those things which he found by experience to be connected in fact, proceeded erroneously to invert this action, and to conclude that association in thought involved similar connexion in reality. (1874: 116)

The key to understanding magic, then, lies in the realisation that natives confuse associations of resemblance and spatio-temporal contiguity with empirical causal connections.[10] There is nothing in reality that connects the crowing rooster with the rising of the sun but because the two events are temporally contiguous, natives assume that by making the rooster crow, they will cause the sun to rise. Nor is there anything in reality that connects ritual dancing with rain, but because the magician moves in ways that resemble rain, natives believes that the dance will induce it.

Such, according to Tylor, is the way in which the occult sciences work, in contrast, but also in an important sense parallel to the sciences proper – parallel because, for Tylor, the aim of both was to achieve practical results. The difference is that while in natural science connections in thought reflect connections in fact, in magical practices they do not. There was nothing mysterious about magic, then, nothing incomprehensible or extraordinary about the people who believed and practised it. If anything, Tylor argued, magic was the product of a rather precocious poetic imagination. To be sure, this was not quite the same thing as the poet's imagination. For even though the poetic mind constructs imaginary worlds as well, at no point does it mis-understand them for reality. Poets are well aware that what they do is poetry, natives are not.[11] Having said that, Tylor made another distinction, this time to defend natives against those Europeans who persisted in the practice of magic. The latter, Tylor argues, are simply ignorant. Even though they are intellectually mature and therefore capable of seeing the light of truth, they refuse to do so. Natives, on the other hand, have not yet reached that stage of intellectual maturity and must not be expected to know what their rational faculties are not ready to grasp. Rather than being ignorant, therefore, natives are innocent like children. Children create imaginary worlds and often behave as if these worlds were real. Unlike ignorant grown-ups, they fall prey to their imagination because at this stage of their intellectual development they do not, and cannot know any better.

Tylor, then, returns to the critical children metaphor that was first employed by the Spanish theologians and missionaries of the sixteenth century. No doubt, his treatment of this metaphor is more sophisticated than that of the Christian ethnologists. Unlike the latter who had no conception of societies evolving and progressing through time, Tylor makes evolution-ism the central tenet of his anthropology. For Tylor natives are not simply like children; they actually represent the 'childhood of the human race' (1874: 248), that is, they occupy a position in the evolution of civilisation analogous to that which children occupy in the life cycle. Nonetheless, Tylor's conclusion is the same as that of his Christian predecessors: given time and guidance, there is nothing to prevent natives from attaining civil-isation. Having been placed in that strange region between the animalistic and the human – the sub-human – natives are now elevated, once again, through the children metaphor to the status of the ab-original – the human of an earlier period. What was thought to be a natural difference and therefore an irrevocable condition now emerges as a purely temporal, and hence redeemable difference.

TWENTIETH-CENTURY PARADIGMS

Malinowski begins his well-known essay on 'Magic, science, and religion' with the following statement:

There are no peoples however primitive without religion and magic. But nor are there, it must be added at once, any savage races lacking either in the scientific attitude or in science, though this lack has been frequently attributed to them. (1948 [1925]: 17)

In this, Malinowski both follows in Tylor's footsteps and departs from him in significant respects. Much like Tylor, he is concerned with countering the perennial claim that some societies are so primitive as to have no religion at all. But unlike him, Malinowski is prepared to locate in Other societies what was considered during his time, and perhaps still is, as the most distinguishing characteristic of the self, namely, science.

This bold step that Malinowski has taken is still the subject of commentary today. Tambiah (1990: 67–8), for example, points out that Malinowski's definition of science 'was both simplistic and generous'. It is true, of course, that Malinowski employed the term in a very broad sense, but whether this is 'simplistic' is a matter of interpretation. It is necessary, at any rate, to bear in mind the context in which Malinowski ventured to define science. His definition was not intended as an explanation of science as such but rather as a tool in defence of Others. In this, he was making use of the same kind of logic that Tylor employed in his own minimalist definition of religion, namely, that broad definitions make manifestations of the self in Other societies much easier to discern. As for Malinowski's 'generosity', it should hardly come to us as a surprise. Even though he could not yet articulate clearly the principle that was to become the basis of subsequent ethnological paradigms – Sameness at the level of cultural value and worth – Malinowski had by this time rejected Tylor's evolutionist project. He was therefore in need of ways and means that would bring the Self and the Other closer together – closer, that is, than Tylor's evolutionary stages ever allowed. In short, unlike Tylor who was still struggling to redeem Others from the calumny of psychological inferiority and save them from de-humanisation, Malinowski was already in the process of smoothing out the rough edges of ethnocentrism.

Tylor's image of native magico-religious systems, according to Malinowski (1948: 18), depicts 'early man' as a philosopher who spends his time contemplating the physical world and the human psyche. Fieldwork 'done by specialists', however, demonstrates than nothing could be more misleading. 'The savage [is] interested rather in his fishing and gardens, in tribal events and festivities'. Far from being a philosopher, he is a practical man immersed in the problems and pleasures of everyday life. In this context, Malinowski also takes on another author, the French philosopher Lévy-Bruhl who denied natives practical rationality or, as Malinowski (1948: 25) put it in a nutshell, claimed that 'primitive man has no sober moods at all, that he is hopelessly and completely immersed in a mystical frame of mind'. It may be useful to explore Lévy-Bruhl's position in greater detail here as a way of anticipating the discussion of Evans-Pritchard's much more detailed critique of the same author below.

Native minds, according to Lévy-Bruhl, operate on a fundamentally different basis from European minds. They are not irrational or illogical, as it is often suggested, but 'pre-logical', that is, at a stage of intellectual development so low that logic itself is not yet possible. The most fundamental characteristic of native mentality, according to Lévy-Bruhl (1925: 38), is mysticism, 'belief in forces and influences and actions which, though imperceptible to sense, are nevertheless [taken to be] real'. Lévy-Bruhl sets up a dichotomy between 'primitive' and 'civilised' minds in terms that are in many ways reminiscent of Hume's stern empiricism. For the French philosopher, however, mysticism is not, as in Hume and Tylor, the outcome of incorrect reasoning proceeding from accurate representation of reality. Rather, it is the result complete lack of reasoning. Natives are unable to reason, according to Lévy-Bruhl, because they have no representations to reason with. Instead of concepts, all they are capable of at their stage of social and intellectual development are images of the world, immediate perceptions in which the distinction between what is perceived and the observer who does the perceiving is not yet possible.

For Lévy-Bruhl, then, natives 'participate' in the world, that is, they exist in a way that does not allow them to conceptualise themselves as entities at once in, and also distinct from the world. By way of explanation, it is often pointed out in the literature of the exotic that in certain native societies people believe their shadow to be their soul. For the French philosopher, however, such statements are an inaccurate description of native mentality. Natives cannot believe anything of the sort because belief presupposes concepts and ideas, which they lack by definition. For Lévy-Bruhl, it would be more accurate to say that when natives see their shadows, they are aware in an immediate and direct way of their souls.

Malinowski's response to Lévy-Bruhl's thesis was not to deny that natives held mystical beliefs and engaged in related practices. Rather, it was to point out that such practices are confined to situations where the natives are unable to control the outcome of their actions. Thus, to use a well-known example, while fishing in the lagoon, the Trobrianders rely exclusively on their practical knowledge and skills. Fishing in the open sea, however, which is 'full of danger and uncertainty', involves 'extensive magical rituals to secure safety and good results' (Malinowski 1948: 31). The fishing example deploys and puts into effective use two strategies of redemption simultaneously. On the one hand, it locates in Trobriand society, if not science as such, certainly a healthy dose of practical rationality. On the other, it deals with the

Otherness of magic in a way that makes it appear 'logical and sensible', as Metcalf would say. The Trobrianders do not engage in magical practices for no apparent reason; they do so only when they have no other outlet. Given their state of technological development, they have no way of ensuring either their safety or a good catch. If they should engage in deep-sea fishing, as they must, they need to find some way to shore up their optimism and to combat uncertainty and fear. Magic is the mechanism that achieves both. Surely, Europeans would resort to similar means under similar circumstances. After all, no one can live without optimism and hope.

The last argument is only implicit in Malinowski's account but a decade later Evans-Pritchard would articulate it in no uncertain terms. The work of Evans-Pritchard is critical for the purposes of the present discussion because it acts as a link between the functionalist paradigm of his time and the symbolic, culturalist paradigms that developed a few decades later. Indeed, his confrontation with Lévy-Bruhl and exposition of Zande witchcraft show that Evans-Pritchard had one foot in functionalism and the other in symbolic interpretation. Much like Malinowski, Evans-Pritchard was concerned with locating in Other societies what for Lévy-Bruhl was the fundamental characteristic of logical mentality – practical rationality. Beyond empirical evidence to this effect, which by this time and as a result of fieldwork was overwhelming and indisputable, Evans-Pritchard makes a strong argument on logical grounds as well. Given the circumstances under which most natives live, Evans-Pritchard points out, it is hardly possible for them to lead a life enveloped in mysticism. They cannot afford to indulge in such fanciful behaviour because, unlike Europeans, 'they live closer to the harsh realities of nature, which permit survival only to those who are guided in their pursuits by observation, experiment and reason' (1965: 87–8).

Natives, then, have a practical orientation to life by necessity, since a sound knowledge of the physical world is the precondition for their very survival. This, of course, is not to say that they do not also hold mystical beliefs and engage in related behaviour. But to the extent that such beliefs and practices may be labelled 'irrational', they are hardly the prerogative of native societies. Drawing on the work of the Italian sociologist Pareto, Evans-Pritchard (1965: 97) argues that the most fundamental European institutions are themselves based on the same sort of irrationalism. 'Theology, metaphysics, socialism, parliaments, democracy, universal suffrage, republics, progress ... are quite as irrational as anything primitives believe in'; they are irrational, according to Evans-Pritchard, because they too 'are the product of faith and sentiment, and not of experiment and reasoning'. Nor is this all. The same sort of thing can be said about 'most of our ideas and actions: our morals, our loyalties to our families and countries and so forth'. If we look at ourselves historically, Evans-Pritchard continues, we will discover that 'we may be a little more critical and sensible than we used to be, but not so much as to make a big difference'. Indeed, 'the relative areas of the logico-experimental and the non-logico-experimental are fairly constant throughout history and in all societies'.

Here, then, we encounter, once again, another deployment of the first two strategies that seek to redeem Others in the eyes of their Western observers and critics. Polarising claims and arguments are undermined and the distance that separates West and Other is reduced. In Evans-Pritchard's account, natives no longer appear to be hopelessly immersed in mysticism and magic, nor do European societies any longer appear to be an exclusively rational domain of thought and action. In his account, the self manifests itself in the Other through the natives' practical orientation in the world and the Other emerges in the West through Western institutions, beliefs, morals, discourses and practices.

Yet Evans-Pritchard was not content to simply demonstrate the pragmatic side of native life and the 'irrationality' of most European institutions and value systems. And with good reason. Belief in democracy or progress may be irrational but this, one could argue, does not automatically make it of the same order as belief in witchcraft. It is one thing to believe that democracy is a good form of government and to have faith in it, even if an unjustifiable one, and quite another to believe that the world is inhabited by mysterious forces that unleash themselves at will and attack their unsuspecting victims. Democratic processes, if not democracy itself, are observable and tangible, spirits are not. It was therefore necessary for Evans-Pritchard to find ways of dealing with the Otherness of magic directly. More specifically, the task before him was to demonstrate that what appeared to be irrational beliefs and practices were in fact sensible ways of coping with universal predicaments. It is precisely this task that Evans-Pritchard undertakes in his famous discussion of Zande witchcraft. Caught in the functionalist paradigm of his time, he sets out to analyse witchcraft from an 'objective' point of view, to examine, that is, how it contributes to the reproduction of Zande society. But Evans-Pritchard was equally interested in the 'subjective' side of witchcraft, the way in which the Azande used it in their everyday lives. I shall turn to the 'objective' aspect of witchcraft first, reversing the order that Evans-Pritchard actually followed, in order to make the transition between him and the writers that followed smoother.

From the 'objective' point of view, witchcraft is nothing but an illusion. This does not mean, however, Evans-Pritchard is quick to point out, echoing Durkheim's argument on religion, that it has no foundation in reality at all. 'Witches, as the Zande conceive them, clearly cannot exist' (Evans-Pritchard 1976 [1937]: 18), but there is a sense in which witches do exist and are as real as anything else we know. In this sense, which is not available to the actors involved, witches are all those individuals who transgress moral codes and engage in anti-social behaviour – the spiteful, 'glum and ill-tempered ... [those] whose habits are dirty ... [the] unmannerly ... [those] who cannot disguise their greed ... who make offensive remarks to their wives and neighbours and fling insults and curses after them' (1976: 52). Belief in witchcraft operates in a way that forces such individuals to curb their anti-social habits and hence diffuses friction and conflict. No one wants to be labelled a witch, and no one wants to be bewitched by others by giving offence to them. Witchcraft, then, Evans-Pritchard points out, is first of all the idiom that the Zande use to speak about anti-social behaviour. More importantly, it is also the system that guarantees the Zande moral order and in this way contributes to the cohesion and stability of Zande society itself. In short, it is a sensible, even if different response to a universal human need – the need, that is, for moral and social order.

Beyond its 'objective' function, witchcraft had a 'subjective' role to play as well. Beyond the universal need for moral and social order, it fulfilled another equally fundamental requirement – the need to make sense of the world that one lives in. Witchcraft, according to Evans-Pritchard, helps the Azande account for the arbitrary and the absurd, for random events and accidents that cause them pain and suffering. It helps them explain such events in a way that makes them socially relevant, meaningful and hence manageable. With this argument Evans-Pritchard establishes a fundamental ethnological theme to which the subsequent generation of scholars – from Lévi-Strauss to Mary Douglas, Turner and Geertz – would return and use in their own work.

In his confrontation with Lévy-Bruhl, Evans-Pritchard argues that the French philosopher failed to make a distinction between perceptual and conceptual analogies. When, for example, the Azande say that a cucumber is an ox, it is not because they perceive it as such. Rather, in a sacrificial situation, the cucumber becomes a symbolic substitute for an ox. The Zande never say that an ox is a cucumber, since the initial claim is a conceptual analogy and not a statement that results from perceptual confusion. But why use such analogies at all? Beyond their obvious practical function, conceptual analogies help the Azande explain otherwise inexplicable and paradoxical events. To use another often-quoted example, in Zandeland, old granaries often collapse and sometimes people are sitting underneath them and get injured. Whenever something of the sort happens, the Azande attribute it to witchcraft. They claim that their injured relatives have been bewitched. The point that scholars such as Lévy-Bruhl fail to see, Evans-Pritchard argues, is that such mystical explanations do not necessarily preclude or contradict other explanations based on observation and empirical causation. Rather, witchcraft explanations are offered over and above the empirical ones. The Azande are well aware that old granaries collapse because termites eat away their foundations. But this does not account for the timing of the event.

Why should these particular people have been sitting under this particular granary at the particular moment when it collapses? That it should collapse is easily intelligible, but why should it have collapsed at the particular moment when these particular people were sitting beneath it? Through the years it might have collapsed, so why should it fall just when certain people sought its kindly shelter? (Evans-Pritchard 1976: 22)

What the Azande wish to understand, then, is the arbitrary nature of such events. We, Evans-Pritchard points out, say that there is no connection between the collapse of the granary and the decision of certain people to sit underneath it. We say that their injury is an accident. But the Azande are not satisfied with this sort of explanation and seek a link between the two events. This link is witchcraft. It does not substitute what the Azande already know – that it is termites that cause the granary's collapse. Rather, it makes what they already know meaningful. Termites do not have intentions, but witches do. The Zande can now search for the witch among their fellow villagers and take action to avenge the injury of their relatives.

Once again, then, Otherness is shown to have form but no content. There is neither confusion between cause and effect in accusations of witchcraft nor are the Zande children of mere fancy given over to mysticism. Witchcraft is simply an idiom or a symbolic system, as ethnographers would say today, that the Azande use to make sense of arbitrary and meaningless events. What appears to be an irrational system of belief and practice emerges in Evans-Pritchard's account as a sensible and necessary one. It emerges as a strategy for coping with misfortune that 'we' ourselves would probably employ under similar circumstances.

And so the story of the salvation intent continues in the 1950s and 1960s with the emergence of new ideas and paradigms or the re-articulation of older ones, but always on the basis of the three strategies of redemption first employed by the Spanish missionaries and theologians of the sixteenth century. The next major ethnological figure that I shall consider, Lévi-Strauss, constructs an argument that combines the first and third redemptive strategies, that is, one that both locates manifestations of the self in the Other and tries to purify Otherness at the same time. In what is perhaps his most influential work, *The Savage Mind*, Lévi-Strauss sets out to locate in native societies what the West prides itself on for being its own unique achievement – science. He does so, not by trying to uncover some previously unnoticed scientific belief or practice, but by a bold and radical reinterpretation of the paradigmatic form of Otherness itself – magico-religious systems. His aim is not to make the moderate claim, by now a commonplace in ethnological writings, that magico-religious practices are a sensible and necessary response to some universal human predicament. It is rather to show that the thought on which such practices are based has been completely misunderstood, and that it is in fact a science in its own right – 'the science of the concrete'.

If after Malinowski and Evans-Pritchard, there remained any doubt about the pragmatic orientation of native societies toward the physical world, Lévi-Strauss's work comes as an additional confirmation. *The Savage Mind* is replete with examples of the detailed knowledge that natives have of nature, particularly of animals and plants. Yet Lévi-Strauss's aim is somewhat different. It is not so much to show that natives have such knowledge to begin with, and that they are therefore practical people, as to demonstrate that, in acquiring this knowledge, they are motivated by concerns that often go far beyond those dictated by sheer physical survival.

The accusation that natives are incapable of rising above the level of basic biological need, above nature and on to the higher level of culture, is as old as the history of Western colonisation of the world. In the beginning of this century, for instance, Malinowski (1922: 61) was still concerned with exposing the myth of the 'shadowy Primitive Economic Man', the 'man', that is, who is solely guided by the desire to satisfy his basic needs. The Kula ring served as Malinowski's primary example of the 'primitive *cultural* man'. The Trobrianders exchange things of no practical use or economic value, but which are nonetheless highly prized in cultural terms. In a similar vein, Lévi-Strauss (1966:3) is concerned with exposing 'the mistake of thinking that the Savage is governed solely by organic or economic need'. He too wants to demonstrate that native interests extend well beyond the natural and on to the higher domain of culture. Lévi-Strauss therefore spends the first pages of *The Savage Mind* trying to convince the reader that natives are interested in animals and plants that 'are of no direct use to them' (1966: 4), that species 'are not known as a result of their usefulness [but] are deemed to be useful or interesting because they are first of all known' (1966: 9). For Lévi-Strauss, this knowledge suggests that natives do not merely consider animals and plants as food, but also as food for thought.

It is true, of course, that native thought is couched in magico-religious, mythical terms that often imply the anticipation of practical results. But this idiom, Lévi-Strauss (1966: 9) argues, should not mislead us into assuming that such results are its only or even primary aim.

> The real question is not whether the touch of a woodpecker's beak does in fact cure toothache. It is rather whether there is a point of view from which a woodpecker's beak and a man's tooth can be seen as 'going together' (the use of this congruity for therapeutic purposes being only one of its possible uses).

In other words, the associations that magical thought establishes are not necessarily prescriptions for practical use, as Victorians anthropologists thought, but primarily logical tools for the creation of theoretical constructs. Lévi-Strauss makes a similar case about myth. If natives myths emerge as fanciful, imaginary tales with no possible basis in reality, it is only because ethnographers approach them from the point of view of historical accounts. The myths' aim, however, is not to tell a story as such, but to explain what actually happened in the past – how and why it happened. Indeed, what is characteristic of myths, Lévi-Strauss argues, is that they have the same fundamental structure the world over and that, as stories, they are simple, predictable and quite impoverished. But this is precisely because their role is 'demarcative rather than aetiological; they do not really explain an origin or indicate a cause; what they do is to invoke an origin or cause (*insignificant in itself*), to make the most of some detail or to "stress" a species'. In short, the aim of myth is 'to establish a difference as a difference' and on the basis of such distinctions to construct systems of logical relations (1966: 230–1).

The theoretical constructs that the 'the savage mind' sets up on the basis of the elements contained in magical and mythical accounts are systems of classification. They are ways of framing and stabilising a world that appears to be in permanent flux, structures that organise the world conceptually and create order out of chaos. The need for conceptual order is of course hardly unique to 'the savage mind'; it is a universal human need. Not only is it universal, but it also lies at the basis of all scientific endeavour. Indeed, as far as Lévi-Strauss is concerned, the process of classification by which the human mind creates a conceptually ordered and stable world constitutes the most fundamental characteristic of science.

On the basis of this critical assumption about the nature of science, Lévi-Strauss is able to transform magical thought into a scientific system. Not that he failed to point out the differences between Western science and native magic, but these he believed to be methodological rather than differences of substance. Western science, according to Lévi-Strauss, classifies the world on the basis of intellectual abstractions, while native magic, being 'the science of the concrete', uses as its building blocks the qualities of observable entities such as plants and animals. In other words, science builds classifications by employing concepts, magic by using 'an intermediary between images and concepts, namely signs' (1966: 18). These differences, according to Lévi-Strauss, do not make magic an earlier, less developed or inferior form of science. Rather, both are 'strategic levels at which nature is accessible to scientific enquiry: one roughly adapted to that of perception and the imagination: the other one at a remove from it' (1966: 15). Even though magic and science are different, then, they are also the Same. They are the Same at the level of cultural value and worth, since both classify the things of the world and create conceptual order equally effectively.

Lévi-Strauss's definition of science has been criticised for focusing on classification without taking account of the notions of cause and effect. As one commentator characteristically put it, 'even Durkheim saw causality as the basic paradigm of scientific knowledge' (Morris 1987: 281). Whatever the value of this criticism, however, we must not lose sight of the fact that Lévi-Strauss's ultimate aim was not to provide a definition of science for science's sake, but a definition that could function as a bridge between self and Other. As I have already pointed out, Tylor employed a similar strategy in his minimalist definition of religion and so did Malinowski in his own 'generous' definition of science. Much like these writers, Lévi-Strauss wants to locate in Other societies what he considers as a fundamental manifestation of the self. He wants to do so because his ultimate aim is to save Others from the calumny of cultural inferiority. Hence, the elasticity of definition.

A few years after the publication of *The Savage Mind*, another major contribution to the effort of redeeming the Otherness of magical thought appeared, Mary Douglas' classic *Purity and Danger*. As Morris (1987: 204–5) points out, in this book Douglas 'is anxious to counter the notion that there is a wide gulf separating our own culture from that of preliterate people, especially the theory that "primitive" people do not make any distinction between ideas of holiness and defilement'. Douglas's 'anxiety' about the imputed gulf between self and Other is of course understandable. What may not be as readily apparent is how this division is sustained by the claim that Others conflate the holy and the unclean. What do holiness and uncleanness have to do with cultural value? And why does the conflation between the two operate as a marker of cultural inferiority? Even though not clearly articulated, the answer to this question is found in the opening pages of Douglas's book.

The conflation between the holy and the unclean, Douglas (1966: 1) points out, is related to an imputed 'fear, terror or dread' of the supernatural, to the concomitant inhibition of reason that fear effects and to the behavioural 'peculiarities' that could develop as a result of such a repression. These alleged 'peculiarities' in native behaviour are nothing other than the various prohibitions and pollution taboos that Douglas examines in her book. Not surprisingly, then, what is at stake here, as elsewhere, what Douglas sets out to repudiate in her analysis of the concepts of pollution and taboo, is the alleged irrationality of magical thought.

Douglas begins her discussion by pointing out that the idea that natives do not make a distinction between the holy and the unclean originates in nineteenth-century anthropology which employed it to buttress its evolutionary claims. More specifically, the idea was used to sustain the distinction between magic and religion and the belief that magic is historically prior to religion and hence characteristic of the lowest levels of civilisation. The holy and the unclean, according to the evolutionist argument, merge only in societies with a magical orientation towards the physical world, where nature is still inhabited by unpredictable and often malevolent supernatural forces and where contact with the unclean, such as corpses and menstrual blood, is thought to bring people perilously close to such forces. This conflation signifies a cultural and intellectual condition where purity and impurity are still conceived of in literal terms, where 'rules of uncleanness pay attention to the material circumstances of an act and judge it good or bad accordingly' (Douglas 1966: 11). This is in contrast to the metaphysical systems of more developed societies where the rules 'disregard material circumstances and judge according to the motives and disposition of the agent', that is, where purity and impurity are understood in ethical terms as a 'spiritual state of unworthiness' (1966: 11). In the last analysis, then, the distinction between those societies that conflate the holy and the unclean and those that keep them separate is a distinction between 'magical, nonethical superstition' (Douglas 1966: 25) and, as Max Weber would say, rationalised religion based on moral principles of conduct.

It is about this imputed gulf, then, that Mary Douglas is 'anxious'. She wants to redeem magical thought but her approach is not to argue, as one might expect, that magic is a rational, moral system like religion. Rather, it is to treat both magic and religion as symbolic expressions, on the one hand, of the conceptual organisation of the world and, on the other, of underlying social realities. In this she follows Durkheim quite closely. Unlike Durkheim, however, who saw in social reality only bonds of solidarity, she sees in addition social divisions and antagonisms. Indeed, for Douglas pollution and taboo are precisely expressions of such divisions. But Douglas goes further than Durkheim in another respect as well. For Durkheim, native religious symbolism reflected a sort of cognitive alienation from the truth of their social conditions. As far as he was concerned, in a rational society people did not need the mediating and obfuscating presence of religion to come to terms with the moral forces that shape them. Indeed, for Durkheim, knowledge of the true provenance of moral rules was the very basis for individual autonomy and freedom.

Durkheim, then, draws a radical distinction between the allegedly rational Western world and a symbolic, alienated Other. Douglas finds this distinction completely unfounded. 'Are our ideas hygienic where theirs are symbolic?' she asks. 'Not a bit of it: I am going to argue that our ideas of dirt also express symbolic systems and that the difference between pollution behaviour in one part of the world and another is a matter of detail' (1966: 34–5). Much like Lévi-Strauss, Douglas is employing two strategies of redemption in one and the same argument. First, she tries to redeem ideas of impurity and pollution by purifying their Otherness – by arguing, that is, that they are nothing more than a symbolic expression of conceptual and social disorder, the idiom with which people come to terms with unclassifiable things and intractable social contradictions. At the same time, and with the same move, she locates this alleged characteristic of Otherness – symbolic, and hence mediated and obfuscating thought – squarely within Western societies themselves.

Even though Western ideas about dirt are influenced by 'our' knowledge of pathogenic organisms, Douglas points out, dirt is still for the West largely a symbolic phenomenon. Take the example of shoes: under the bed, they are not dirty, but become so as soon as they are placed on the kitchen table; or the example of a sheet of paper on the desk that automatically becomes litter when thrown in the street. Dirt is 'matter out of place', which is to say, a matter of order and disorder – conceptual, spatial and social disorder – rather than something that has to do with sickness and disease. 'We' avoid it, as much as 'they' do, not so much because it threatens our health as because it threatens order; 'it involves no special distinction between primitives and moderns: we are all subject to the same rules [of avoidance]' (1966: 40). Dirt is anything that contradicts and undermines systems of classification, whether 'ours' or 'theirs', and hence threatens the stability of the social world.[12]

What remains to be shown, then, is how Douglas uses the idea of dirt-as-symbol to redeem the Otherness of pollution and taboo. I shall do so by discussing two of her own examples. The first, well-known example has to do with eating taboos and refers to the biblical view that the pig is an abomination and hence unfit for human consumption. This taboo, Douglas (1966: 49) points out, has nothing to do with 'hygiene, aesthetics, morals and instinctive revulsion', much less with irrational superstition. Rather, it expresses the fact that this particular animal does not conform fully to its class, namely, domesticated, cloven-hoofed, cud-chewing animals. The pig, being cloven-hoofed but not ruminant, is on the basis of this classification a hybrid, and its hybridity makes it an abomination. Douglas (1966: 55) generalises the point by arguing that the 'underlying principle of cleanness in animals is that they shall conform fully to their class'. Animal classes and systems of classification are of course cultural constructs and in this sense quite arbitrary. As Douglas points out, the category of cloven-hoofed, cud-chewing animals reflects the importance that the ancient Israelis attached to the cow. Any form of classification, however, is better than no classification at all, any conceptual ordering of the world, no matter how inadequate, is better than chaos. Thus, the assumption with which Douglas operates – in tune with Lévi-Strauss and Geertz – is that 'it is part of our human condition to long for hard lines and clear concepts' (1966: 162). For it is with such lines and concepts that we frame the world and organise our lives. Hence the fact that whatever contradicts our systems of classification emerges as a danger to be suppressed or avoided. At the level of eating habits, this sort of danger is expressed symbolically by designating certain animals as unclean and hence unfit for human consumption.

The second example I have chosen refers to contradictions in the social order rather than in the order of classifications. It has to do with the notion of sexual pollution, particularly as a result of coming into contact with menstrual blood. The notion is widespread among New Guinea tribes, according to Douglas, but it is particularly pronounced among the Mae Enga. In this tribe 'there is a strongly held belief that contact with women weakens male strength' (1966: 147). So strong is this belief, in fact, that even within marriage sexual intercourse is reduced 'to the minimum necessary for procreation'. This may strike outsiders as nothing more than an irrational fear, but, as Douglas is at pains to point out, the taboo is an expression of the social conflicts embedded in Enga society. The latter consists of exogamous clans that compete fiercely for prestige and power, which means in effect that every marriage is based on enmity. Men must marry women from outside their clan, that is, from clans that they consider as their traditional enemies. In their pollution beliefs and sexual avoidance, the Enga are trying to overcome symbolically a fundamental social contradiction – the fact that they must marry their enemies and build a family on hate relations.

There is, then, a rational explanation for bizarre pollution ideas and beliefs, whether ideas about food, sex or anything else for that matter. Indeed, far from being superstitions, taboos are 'creative' and 'positive' (Douglas 1966: 2) responses to a universal human predicament – the need to maintain a conceptual grip on a world which is inherently slippery and unruly. With this explanation, the Otherness of pollution and taboo is redeemed; it ceases to be Other and becomes the Same. In their beliefs and practices – say, their abhorrence of pork – we can now begin to recognise our own pollution-related behaviour – for example, our abhorrence of eating cats and dogs (Sahlins 1977). In them, we can now begin to see our own selves.

No discussion of magico-religious beliefs and practices would be complete without mention of Geertz's seminal essay 'Religion as a Cultural System' (1973b). In this essay Geertz sets out to invigorate the discipline and to transcend what he perceives as the theoretical stagnation in the study of religion. There is no doubt, however, that the essay makes an important contribution, not only to theory but also to the long-standing effort to redeem the Otherness of magico-religious systems. As Asad (1993: 50) observes, 'the separation of religion from science, common sense, aesthetics, politics, and so on, allows [Geertz] to defend it against charges of irrationality'. Like all ethnographers, then, and by his own admission, Geertz (1973a: 36) upholds 'the governing principle of the field' – a principle that, as he argues, should 'not be turned into an empty phrase'. This principle is none other than 'the basic unity of mankind'.

As is well known, Geertz argues that religion – a term he uses to refer to magico-religious beliefs and practices in general[13] – is a cultural system. In keeping with his general theory of culture, Geertz (1973b: 92) defines cultural systems as 'extrinsic sources of information' responsible 'for the institution of the social and psychological processes which shape behaviour'. As I have already suggested, the argument repeats, even if in a more elaborate and explicit way, the claims that Lévi-Strauss and Mary Douglas have already made about the human condition. Having tried the cultural way, human beings can no longer depend on the mute certainty of instinct. In order to survive, they have no option but to rely on their own devices, the 'extrinsic sources of information' they have developed and encoded in symbols, namely, culture. Geertz's argument, however, goes beyond Lévi-Strauss and Mary Douglas in his emphasis on meaning – not merely semantic but also, and more importantly, existential meaning. Religion is no longer that system of categories that organises the natural and social world in an intelligible way. It is rather, in addition, what provides answers to troublesome, perennial questions about the nature of the human condition and of human destiny. In short, it is what makes an inherently indifferent world meaningful and bearable. Geertz, then, returns to the scene of the Zande granaries where Evans-Pritchard left the thread, picks it up and brings it forward onto a much larger stage – 'the problem of meaning' writ large.

There are three points at which meaninglessness can break in on 'man' and overturn his life, according to Geertz (1973b: 100). The first has to do with the human ability to know the world, to distinguish, that is, between what is true and what is false. Human beings need to be convinced that there is such a thing as the truth and that, if not yet known, it is nonetheless ultimately knowable. The contrary 'sets ordinary human experience in a permanent context of metaphysical concern and raises the dim, back-of-the-mind suspicions that one may be adrift in an absurd world' (1973b: 102). The second breaking point is that of emotional endurance and has to do with the meaninglessness of human suffering. The point is not to put an end to personal suffering and loss because this is an unattainable goal. It is rather to make sense of suffering, to understand why it is an inescapable part of life, and by understanding it to make it bearable. Last, there is 'the problem of evil' that poses a threat 'to our ability to make sound moral judgements' (1973b: 105–6). Once again, the question is not how to do away with evil – with injustice or inequality – but to explain why such things exists at all. In short, in addition to the need for making intellectual and emotional sense of the world, there is, according to Geertz, also a need for making moral sense. Religion is precisely the instrument that caters for all three needs. Whenever people reach the point where the suspicion arises that life may be after all 'absurd and the attempt to make moral, intellectual, or emotional sense of experience ... bootless', religion intervenes; and 'by means of symbols', it furnishes people in existential distress with 'an image of such a genuine order of the world which will account for, and even celebrate, the perceived ambiguities, puzzles, and paradoxes in human experience' (1973b: 108).

With Geertz, anthropology has come a long way from the point where magical thought appeared as the product of feeble and innocent minds, an irrationalism characteristic of the lowest stages of civilisation. This paradigmatic form of Otherness has become so familiar to 'us' now that it can no longer be considered strange or alien. It is how Other people ritualise optimism and hope – and do 'we' not have the Same need as well, and meet this need through our own rituals? It is also a mechanism that curbs antisocial behaviour and contributes to the maintenance of the social order – and what could be more necessary in any society, our own included, than order itself? It is a conceptual device that Other people use to arrest the flux of impressions and to construct a stable world around them – and do we not ourselves transform perceptual and conceptual chaos into a cosmos, an ordered and organised universe? Last, this form of Otherness proclaims that whatever in the world escapes human attempts to understand and explain, it can still be comprehended and explained, that there is always a larger picture in which even the most absurd of things make sense – and could we ourselves do without such an auspicious message, could we ever survive in an arbitrary, senseless and indifferent world? In this Otherness, then, which is no longer Other but the Same, we now see ourselves. It is true that it requires some effort to realise that it is really us that we see in them, but once we drop our prejudices and misconceptions there can hardly be any doubt: they are essentially and fundamentally the Same as us!

Such, at any rate, is the world as the ethnographer desires and imagines it – devoid of Otherness, symbolically unified and ethically meaningful, a world of human purity and pure humanity. Yet the ethnological story of the salvation intent is not a story of salvation. It is certainly not the story of the happy re-assimilation of the Other by the Same. It is not even the story of partial unification, which means that this is not the end of the story – neither the end of the salvation intent itself nor of the story that the present discourse has been narrating. There is still more to be said because there is more that has been, and is being done to save Others. Despite decades of effort, the three strategies of redemption and the innumerable instances of their deployment notwithstanding, Otherness is still out there, as much beyond the ethnographer's reach as it has ever been, and haunts the eth-nological imagination with vengeance. And because it is still out there, there is widespread uneasiness and discontent within the discipline. There are loud dissenting voices that not only denounce the existence of this profanity, but also speak accusingly of the ethnographers' share of responsibility for this state of affairs. These voices belong to heterodox ethnographers and constitute the latest in the perennial, and perennially unsuccessful attempt to save the Other.

THE ETHNOLOGICAL COMPLICITY

Much has been said in the discipline about the so-called 'postmodern' by both proponents and opponents but there is hardly any need to repeat it here.[14] I would rather point to something that has been largely overlooked, namely, a certain assumption that underscores both the orthodox and heterodox views. The assumption is that the 'postmodern' somehow transcends modernity and announces a new era in anthropology, whether one to be welcomed because, as heterodox ethnographers would argue, it promises to liberate both the discipline's practitioners from their illusions and Others from the power that ethnological discourse exercises over them; or an era to be denounced because, as orthodox ethnographers would argue, it threatens to put an end to science and objectivity, even to the discipline itself.

Dramatic as they are, such arguments should not be taken at face value. Far from going beyond the modern, heterodox discourse is more consistently modern than modernity itself. A similar argument about the 'postmodern' in general has been recently put forward by the theorists of 'reflexive mod-ernisation', Anthony Giddens (1990) and Ulrich Beck (1992). And although there is much to disagree about with these authors – not least because they are both apologists of modernity and hence defenders of a privileged identity – on this issue, they are far more perceptive than the proponents of ethno-logical modernity. These theorists are perceptive enough to see that what is fundamental about modernity is not science as such, but rather a certain logic that may be closely related to, but is certainly not exhausted by science.

Giddens and Beck call this logic 'reflexivity', meaning, in the broadest possible terms, becoming aware of the conditions of possibility of Being. To place it in its proper historical and cultural context, I call it the logic that objectifies and, as Max Weber would say, disenchants the world.

I shall have more to say about reflexivity in the next chapter, where I will discuss at length how heterodox discourse employs this logic in its critical disenchanting of orthodox anthropology. Here, it should suffice to say that the most fundamental characteristic of this mode of thought is its propensity to turn beings into objects for the human subject, and to reduce their mode of existence to this one-dimensional relationship. In contrast to other ways of thinking, where beings are often said to have an independent and autonomous existence, this logic recognises them only insofar as they are objects, that is, under the subject's cognitive and potentially practical control. Hence the notion of disenchantment or de-magification of the world, that is, its transformation from an animated to a mechanical universe. At the limit, this logic makes Being itself the product of human existence, a historical (or social or cultural) construct, and, by extension, the human subject the Creator of the world.

In anthropology, the 'postmodern' repeats modernity in another significant respect which will be the subject of discussion in these concluding remarks. Let us first note what has already been said, namely, that heterodox discourse is striving to achieve what has been the primary objective of all twentieth-century anthropology – the redemption of Otherness and the unification of the world at the symbolic level. Let us also note the way in which heterodox discourse goes about this task. The argument that it has developed to redeem Otherness follows the logic of the first strategy of redemption – the strategy, that is, which locates manifestations of the self in Other societies. If there is a difference from earlier paradigms, it is only that heterodox discourse takes the argument to its logical extreme.

In order to buttress the claim that the self manifests itself in native societies, ethnographers deploying the first redemptive strategy must explain why other observers of native life, whether from within the discipline or from outside, overlook such manifestations. In many cases, this involves a certain critique of representation. As I have already suggested, Tylor criticised his contemporaries for using too restricted a definition of religion to be able to observe native religious institutions – he himself represented religion in the widest possible terms. For their part, Malinowski and Lévi-Strauss used quite a broad definition of science for pretty much the same reasons. Heterodox discourse, by contrast, criticises not particular representations – of religion or science, of this or that institution – but representation writ large. The question it raises is not whether certain representations may be too narrow or inaccurate, but rather whether representation as such can ever yield the truth about Others – a question that it emphatically answers in the negative.

As I have already suggested, heterodox discourse presents itself as an epistemological argument concerned with the possibility (or otherwise) of knowing the truth about Others, and it is only indirectly and tacitly that it raises the question of Sameness. Even though the critique of ethnological representation is articulated with an eye on the power that the discipline exercises over Others, and hence is directly involved in the perennial and perennially unsuccessful attempt to redeem Otherness, there is nowhere explicit discussion of the ontological context in which power emerges as a problem to be resolved. In other words, although heterodox ethnographers criticise the discipline for defining Others as 'Other', they nowhere explain *why* the discipline should be criticised for doing what it does. In the last chapter, I argued that as long as heterodox ethnographers maintain that there is a crisis in representation, that is, as long as they present their discourse as a purely epistemological argument, their critique of ethnological orthodoxy rests on very shaky grounds. It runs into the intractable paradox of claiming to know what fiction is without having any knowledge of the truth in relation to which ethnological representations become fiction.

To thematise this paradox is already to uncover the ethnological complicity that makes the heterodox strategy of redemption possible. If heterodox ethnographers can argue that ethnological representations are fiction and get away with this argument – without anyone, that is, pointing out its contradictory nature – it is only because everyone in the discipline takes Sameness for granted.

Sameness is placed beyond questioning by ethnographers. It is placed beyond truth and fiction and functions as the basis on which the truth or falsity of ethnological representations can be decided. The silence that ensues from this complicity allows heterodox ethnographers to play an impossible double role with impunity. It allows them to treat themselves as both epistemological objects and subjects. Heterodox ethnographers can now be both finite epistemological objects caught within society and history and infinite epistemological subjects who are well aware of the limits that society and history impose on knowledge. They can be both ordinary ethnographers who, like everyone else, must inevitably produce partial truths about Others, and post-ethnographers or transhistorical thinking subjects who not only know that it is only partial truths that ethnographers produce but can also explain why this is happening. This makes it possible for heterodox ethnographers to deploy their own impossible redemptive strategy – impossible and doomed to failure because already burdened with an irreconcileable contradiction.

On the face of it, what heterodox ethnographers have done is to argue that every ethnological representation is fiction. In essence, they have only argued that every ethnological representation is fiction *except* the one that must remain unthematised – Sameness. To this representation that goes without saying – because it comes without saying – the heterodox argument does not, and is not meant to apply. The heterodox argument, then, is that fiction that the discipline has been producing throughout its history, namely, Otherness. The implicit consequences of the heterodox argument are quite startling. In the aftermath of the heterodox critique, it becomes possible, once again, to think about Others, but this time the ground has been cleared and there is no danger of pitfalls. Before the advent of heterodox discourse, it was always possible for ethnographers to mistake Otherness for the truth because they had no sense of their epistemological limits. This danger no longer exists. Otherness has been shown to be fiction, an invention of the epistemologically limited ethnological imagination. Ethnographers can now be absolutely certain that Otherness is fiction because there is no doubt that they, like everyone else, are caught within society and history. But if there can be no doubt that Otherness is false, there can hardly be any doubt either about the status of its opposite: Sameness is true. What ethnographers have always known to be the case intuitively is now proven deductively and by default. Paradoxically, Sameness rests solidly on the other side of the ethnological certainty about the limits of representation. Sameness is true because ethnographers, being epistemologically limited, can only produce fictions.

This, then, is the fourth and most recent redemptive strategy to have emerged from a discipline that takes it upon itself to save Others from the West and from its own discourses and practices. This strategy constitutes the so-called 'postmodern turn' in the discipline, but as I have tried to show it is hardly a turn at all. If anything, it is more like an impulsive forward jump, an impatient run towards the very objective that anthropology set for itself so long ago but has never been able to achieve. What remains to be seen is whether heterodox discourse comes any closer to redeeming Others from the calumny of inferiority than the other twentieth-century paradigms. As I have already suggested, and will discuss in greater detail in the next chapter, it comes no closer to this objective and fares no better than anything that preceded it. Ironically, in this sense too, there is little of substance that separates heterodox discourse from the established ethnological orthodoxy. The former does little more than to repeat, ceremoniously so, the monumental failures of the latter. In this sense too, the 'postmodern' and the modern are united in a tight and fateful embrace.

4   WHAT THE NATIVES DON'T KNOW

'Weeping icon moves a nation', began one of the Cyprus News Agency's (CNA) items on the World Wide Web on 7 February 1997. The nation in question is the Greek Cypriot community of this eastern Mediterranean island and the icon a fifteenth-century portrayal of the Virgin and Christ-child at Kykko monastery, high up on the Troodos mountains. The report continues in the same sensationalist manner:

Thousands of faithful worshippers continue to be moved to tears by a phenomenon here that defies scientific explanation. ... [The] icon has been shedding what seem to be thick, fragrant tears non-stop for almost a week now. ... 'We see this as a miracle. From the way it happened, we consider it a miracle. Nothing less nothing more', says Archmandrite Sergios Kykkotis, a monk at Kykko. ... 'Most people go there out of curiosity but leave overwhelmed by the event. The curiosity leaves and the miracle takes over. They accept it as a miracle', Kykkotis told CNA. (CNA 1977a: 2–3)

The local people interpreted the miracle in various ways, according to CNA. For many it was an ominous sign for the future of the island, which has been divided into north and south since the Turkish invasion of 1974. The northern part is under Turkish military occupation and, for many Greek Cypriots the fear, fuelled by frequent Turkish threats (symbolic and otherwise), is that the Turkish troops may begin a new round of hostilities and take over the rest of the island. Others, including the monastery's abbot, appeared more optimistic and suggested that the weeping icon may be an auspicious sign after all. As the abbot reasoned, 'the Virgin is not a "Cassandra" who foreshadows only bad things' (CNA 1997a: 3). A few days later (9 February 1997), CNA reported that the archbishop officiated in prayers at the monastery, an event that was attended by thousands of worshippers. 'It was the first time since 1977, when late Archbishop Makarios III was buried at Throni, near Kykko monastery, that the area has experienced such a throng', continues the second CNA report. 'Cars were immobilised as thousands [of the faithful] passed underneath the icon which was carried in a procession around the Monastery' (CNA 1997b: 2).

This, then, is a story about a miraculous icon.[1] It is about how the divine intervenes in the world, if only to relay an equivocal message – ominous or auspicious, no one can really tell. It is also about how a nation responds to claims of divine intervention – hesitantly at first (is this some kind of a hoax?), but soon, having witnessed the miraculous at first hand, with awe and veneration. In short, this is a story about faith. Not that this sort of faith is as widespread in Cyprus as the CNA's sensational reports suggest. As I pointed out elsewhere (Argyrou 1993), many educated middle-class Cypriots sweep aside the magical and the miraculous with a dismissive wave of the hand. Such things, they argue, are nothing more than superstitions and have no place in a modern, rational society. Nor is this, in fact, the kind of news that the media should be reporting around the world. It gives foreigners the impression that Greek Cypriots still live in the Middle Ages. Indeed, several middle-class acquaintances were dismayed to find out that news of the miracle was reported by CNA on the Web. As one characteristically put it, '*eghinikamen rezili dhiethnos*' (we've become a laughing stock internationally).

In anthropology we think that we have come a long way since the days when the magico-religious operated as a manifestation of cultural inferiority. The ideas of Victorian anthropologists now appear as a sort of superstition themselves and cause contemporary ethnographers embarrassment not unlike that which belief in miracles causes educated, middle-class Cypriots. For ethnographers today, there are no longer innocent, child-like natives, only misinformed Victorian anthropologists who failed utterly to understand the symbolic significance of magico-religious beliefs and practices. Natives, ethnographers argue, do not invoke magic and religion to achieve practical results but, among other things, to make sense of arbitrary events – the fact that granaries collapse and fall on some people and not others (Evans-Pritchard 1976 [1937]), the often inexplicable nature of physical pain (Lévi-Strauss 1963), or the paradoxical situation where the rain falls on the 'just fella ... because the unjust has the just's umbrella' (Geertz 1973b: 106).

No doubt, this sort of interpretation can be applied to the event at Kykko monastery or, at any rate, to those Greek Cypriots who have been 'overwhelmed' by it and 'accept it as a miracle'. They too, one could plausibly argue, seek to make sense of an arbitrary and absurd state of affairs. They live on a small island that has been made even smaller by a long-standing division; many are refugees in their own country, and some can even see their houses and properties in the Turkish-occupied area every day, so near and yet so far beyond their reach. What could be more arbitrary and absurd than that? If religion explains why the unjust fella has the just's umbrella and can get away with it, would not a weeping icon be a sign of some sort, a divine message for the just – and perhaps also the unjust – to heed?

It is possible, then, to interpret the event at Kykko monastery along such lines, but when everything is said and done, how different really would the natives' image be from those that Victorian anthropology constructed? We certainly take it for granted that there is a world of difference between the two. Is it not after all the case, one might ask, that for Victorian anthropology magico-religious practices were irrational? And is it not true also that symbolic interpretation has shown them to be a sensible and necessary responses to universal predicaments? Could there be a greater difference than this? And yet, it seems that we must think again. For it is not at all certain that the symbolic paradigms of the twentieth century have been able to avoid the implication that magico-religious systems are in a certain sense irrational. This may not be the sort of irrationalism posited by Victorian anthropology but nor is it, for this reason, any less pernicious. As Sperber (1975: 8) argues, symbolism 'does not eliminate the problem of irrationality, it only shifts it'. The shift, according to Sperber, is away from the irrationalism of practices that misinterpret the truth of the empirical world to the irrationalism of practices that employ excessive means for the attainment of modest goals. Take, for instance, Lévi-Strauss's interpretation of myth. In order to constitute a simple logical opposition, 'the savage mind' creates an entire, often highly complex story – a story, that is, whose actual content is only tangentially relevant to the task at hand. Indeed, as Lévi-Strauss himself recognises, myths are essentially redundant, since the opposition that they set up can be established with lesser and simpler means. The imbalance between means and ends, and the irrationalism that this entails, Sperber (1975: 8) argues, is even greater in the case of ritual. 'Think of the time, the tension, the passion and the expense necessary to put on the smallest ritual'. If ritual is a symbolic practice, if its aim is to convey some sort of message, it is an exorbitant way of communicating. The message is 'paraphrasable in ordinary language at a comparatively non-existent expense of energy'.[2]

There is, then, a case to be made against the symbolic paradigms of the twentieth century for implicitly positing a certain irrationalism about native magico-religious beliefs and practices. Contrary to all appearances, therefore, there is also a case to be made about a certain degree of affinity between these paradigms and Victorian anthropology. And yet my concern here is with another kind of similarity between Victorian and contemporary ethnographers, and another kind of division between 'us' and 'them' no less fundamental. More specifically, I am interested in the division that ethnographers effect by claiming to know the truth about native life – in this case the truth about magico-religious systems – to which the natives whose life it is are oblivious. My concern is with the practice, in which both Victorian anthropology and all twentieth-century paradigms are implicated, of positing a certain unthought for Others, a sort of cognitive alienation on the natives' part from the 'real' content and 'true' meaning of their lives to which only ethnographers have access.

To say that both Victorian and post-Victorian anthropology are implicated in this practice is not to suggest that the nature of the natives' unconscious that each posits or the imputed causes of this unconscious are the same. For Victorian anthropology, natives use magic to achieve certain practical result – for example, to control rain, the sun or the wind (Frazer 1963 [1922]: 72–96). This is so because they do not quite know how the physical world actually operates, because there is a certain body of empirical knowledge of which they are unaware. As for the causes of this empirical unthought, they are explained in terms of an imputed cognitive inability, even if not inherent, to distinguish between symbol and reality – a conflation that E.B. Tylor dubbed 'direct symbolism'.[3] For their part, twentieth-century paradigms have convincingly shown that when it comes to practical matters, natives are as capable of distinguishing between the real and the ideal as anyone else. They have successfully discredited the empirical unconscious but, as I will argue below in detail, they have done so at the cost of constituting a new domain of native obliviousness – a sociocultural unconscious. In all twentieth-century paradigms natives emerge as those who know the truth of the empirical world, but do not know the truth of their society and culture; as those who can distinguish between symbol and reality in nature, but who are unwilling or unable to do so at the level of sociocultural reality. What, then, is the nature of the sociocultural unconscious as this emerges in ethnological discourse? What is it about society and culture that natives misunderstand, and how is this imputed misunderstanding reflected in their magico-religious beliefs and practices? In short, what is it that magic and religion symbolise?

The history of the discipline provides two broad answers to these questions. In the first place, there is the Durkheimian school of thought that posits a social unconscious in native societies. Magico-religious systems, according to the argument, reflect and contribute to the reproduction of the social order. This may be a unified social order, as Durkheim himself postulated or, more realistically, an order characterised by social divisions and antagonisms, as Evans-Pritchard and Mary Douglas have argued. The point is that natives are oblivious to this truth about their lives – they are oblivious to the 'fact', according to ethnographers at any rate, that the metaphysical forces in magic and religion are nothing other than social forces expressed symbolically. Natives take magic and religion literary, according to the argument, and do not realise that underneath the symbol there is a social reality that is the source of both.

Beyond the social unconscious, twentieth-century anthropology also posits a cultural unconscious in native societies. The story of this unthought begins with Evans-Pritchard in his discussion of Zande witchcraft, continues in the work of Lévi-Strauss and Mary Douglas and culminates in the sort of culturalist anthropology developed by Clifford Geertz. What unifies such diverse writers is the broad claim that native magico-religious systems operate as machines for the production of conceptual order and significance in an otherwise chaotic and indifferent world. Magic and religion resolve contradictions, explain anomalies and make the arbitrary appear necessary and natural. As in the case of the social unconscious, the system is burdened with a very important function, namely, the reproduction of the cultural order. Thus, here too, the truth of magico-religious beliefs and practices must remain hidden from the natives' eyes. This of course is not to say that natives do not suspect the nature of this truth; nor is it in fact the case that they are in principle incapable of articulating it. But they must forget what they know, the ethnological argument suggests, because otherwise the world of significance that this truth, by hiding itself as it does, makes possible will collapse. In other words, magico-religious beliefs would no longer be meaningful ways of making the world meaningful. The Zande would now be forced to tolerate the disturbing idea that there are no intentions behind the collapse of granaries and that the timing of such events is a sheer accident; and the 'just fella' would not only lose hope of ever recovering his umbrella from the 'unjust' but also, and more importantly, would lose hope of ever making sense of injustice.

Tylor's notion of 'direct symbolism', then – the conflation of symbol and reality – informs the assumptions of twentieth-century paradigms and guides their interpretation of native life as much as it guided Tylor himself. Whatever the differences between them, Victorian positivism and contemporary symbolic interpretation are united by this fundamental similarity – fundamental because both paradigms divide the world along the same lines. Ethnographers today claim, as much as their Victorian peers did, to know the truth about Other lives – a truth to which the natives are, and must remain, oblivious. They construct images of native reality, of magico-religious beliefs and practices, in which natives recognise themselves no more and no better than in the images that Victorian anthropology constructed. In short, for both Victorian and post-Victorian anthropology, there is a fundamental distinction to be made – between ethnographers who think the natives' unthought and analyse their unconscious, whether of the empirical or sociocultural variety, and natives who must bear the weight of this dark and silent load without even realising that they are doing so.

This division is as radical and pernicious as that between the rational and the irrational, and I shall have more to say about it in the last section of the present chapter. At this point, it should suffice to say that the truth – which ethnographers know and natives do not – and the process of reflection and doubt by which it is acquired are saturated with cultural value. The truth is inextricably associated with what is perhaps the most cherished of Western ideologies, namely, individual autonomy and freedom. This is freedom not merely from ignorance – not a question, that is, of truth for truth's sake – but also, and more importantly, freedom from the dependence and domination that ignorance entails. It is the freedom of those who have become masters of their lives and make their own history, whether personal or collective, in contrast to those whose lives are subject to outside forces and who are made by history instead. Knowledge of the truth, then, is by means of this association *predisposed* to act as a marker of distinction – predisposed because it distinguishes ('us') and discriminates (against 'them') even when it is not intentionally employed for this purpose. Thus, the higher the cultural premium placed on individual autonomy and freedom in Western societies, the deeper the division that knowledge of the truth effects.

To explore the sociocultural unconscious more fully, it is necessary to return to Durkheim and his classic study *The Elementary Forms of the Religious Life*. For it is from this important work that much of the subsequent ethnological discussion on the topic draws its inspiration. As is well known, Durkheim was highly critical of nineteenth-century intellectuals who viewed religion as sheer 'illusion'. That natives misrecognised the truth of religion, Durkheim did not doubt; that religion was nothing more than a figment of their imagination however, he would not accept. 'A human institution cannot rest upon an error and a lie, without which it could not exist', Durkheim (1976 [1915]: 2) points out. 'If it were not founded in the nature of things, it would have encountered in the facts a resistance over which it could never have triumphed'. For Durkheim, then, there was truth in religion – and a fundamental one at that – even if it was a truth from which the natives themselves were alienated. Although the reasons that natives provide to explain their religious practices are 'erroneous', Durkheim declares, 'the true reasons do not cease to exist, and it is the duty of science to discover them'. For science knows how to 'go underneath the symbol to the reality it represents and which gives it its meaning' (1976: 2–3). No doubt Durkheim's attitude and language strike us as scientistic and dated, but the essence of what he has to say about the symbolism of religion differs very little, if at all, from what the ethnological paradigms of the twentieth century themselves posit.

For Durkheim, then, natives misunderstand the true nature of their religious beliefs and practices because they conflate symbol and reality. For example, they think that animals and plants are deities, but a totem is nothing more than the flag of the tribe; they believe that through sacrifice they are communicating with their gods, when in fact all they are doing is entering into communion with one another. In short, in celebrating supernatural forces, natives are in reality celebrating the forces that tie them together into a moral community. This is the reality 'underneath the symbol' to which they are oblivious, the social unthought that Durkheim is thinking out for them in his book. Religion may be the way in which society becomes conscious of itself, but in Durkheim's account it certainly is not the way in which natives become conscious of themselves as a society. On the contrary, it is a mediating and obfuscating presence, a screen that interposes itself between what they think and what they truly are, a mirror in which their image becomes distorted so much that only an outside observer can recognise it. Durkheim does not posit any inherent inability on the part of natives to come to terms with what they are in a direct and immediate way. But neither is he entirely consistent when he attempts to account for this imputed failure.

In his discussion of totemism, for example, Durkheim raises the question as to 'how it happens that [social] forces are thought of under the form of totems' (1976: 219) and makes two arguments. The first is related to the impact of emotions, the second to the way in which thought processes operate. It would seem that natives begin like everyone else, namely, with a simple act of naming. They give the name of an animal or plant to their clan and from this point onwards the animal or plant becomes their emblem. Up to this point there is no confusion, no conflation of symbol and reality. However, Durkheim continues, 'it is a well-known law that the sentiments aroused in us by something spontaneously attach themselves to the symbol which represents them' (1976: 219). In the midst of ritualistic 'efferves-cence', the emotions aroused by social forces are transferred directly to the totem which is the emblem of the clan. As a result, what appears to generate these emotions is no longer the bonds of solidarity that tie the clan together, but the totem itself. In other words, the totem is no longer the emblem of the clan; it becomes something dissociated from it and assumes an independent existence. It is transformed into a deity. This psychological argument is not very different from that which David Hume employed in the eighteenth century in his discussion of miracles. As we have seen, for Hume it was the existence of 'vulgar' emotions that accounted for belief in miracles. For emotions cloud human reason so that people can no longer distinguish between the thing that they use to represent an idea and the idea itself.

The mistaking of the symbol for what it represents – Tylor's 'direct symbolism' – becomes virtually unavoidable, according to Durkheim (1976: 220), whenever a complex, abstract idea is represented by something simple and concrete. This practice has something to do with the nature of the thinking process itself, particularly, as Durkheim makes clear, the thinking processes of those with low intelligence. To begin with, people find it 'difficult to hold in the mind' the 'thing itself', in this case the notion of the clan, because of 'its dimensions, the number of its parts and the complexity of their arrangement'. They must represent it with something else. People can deal much better with 'concrete object[s] ... [of] whose reality [they] are vividly aware'. Complex and abstract ideas are therefore represented by simple, concrete things and, given the obscurity of the former and the vividness of the latter, the thing eventually becomes the idea itself. We can see this trans-mutation occurring even in our midst, according to Durkheim. We represent the nation with a piece of colourful cloth – the flag – but the soldier who gets killed in the process of trying to save the flag from the enemy, even when the nation is no longer in danger, does not make a distinction between the two. 'He loses sight of the fact that the flag is only a sign, and that it has no value in itself, but only brings to mind the reality that it represents; it is treated as if it were this reality itself' (1976: 220). If soldiers in developed societies fall into the trap of confusing the flag with the nation, it should be understand-able why natives themselves conflate the totem and the clan. 'The clan is too complex a reality to be represented clearly ... by such *rudimentary intelligences*' (1976: 220; my emphasis).

It would appear, then, that for Durkheim there are two factors involved in the conflation of symbol and reality – emotions and the difficulty some people have in thinking complex thoughts directly, that is, without the mediating assistance of simple, concrete things. In the conclusion of his book, however, Durkheim offers yet another explanation of 'direct symbolism'. The discussion is about the contrast between religion and science and Durkheim points out, approvingly, that the former is increasingly being displaced by the latter. And yet, there is also 'something eternal in religion', according to Durkheim (1976: 430), 'the cult and the faith'. The question then becomes why people should need faith during the age of reason, at a time when science increasingly makes significant inroads and illuminates so many previously obscured and ill-understood domains of life. Durkheim's (1976: 431) answer is simple: 'Science is fragmentary and incomplete; it advances but slowly and is never finished; but life cannot wait.' By its very nature, then, life requires answers here and now, and if science cannot provide them, religion certainly can. Thus, 'the theories which are destined to make men live and act are ... obliged to pass science and complete it prematurely' – complete it, that is, in the form of its inferior alter ego, namely, religion.

In this version of Durkheim's argument, which is more relevant for the purposes of the present discussion, people must have faith because they cannot afford to do otherwise. They must believe in an inferior kind of truth – that provided by religion – because they cannot wait for science to discover the 'real' truth. It should be apparent that this distinction is relevant for analytical purposes only. Indeed, as Durkheim suggests, in real life there can be no doubt in the believer's mind about the validity of religious truths. If people doubted the 'premature' truths that religion provides, these truths would be obsolete; they would lack the necessary force that makes 'men live and act'. The symbol, then, must be treated as if it were reality – the power emanating from the clan as if it were emanating from the totem – and any thought that it might not be what it appears to be must be effaced from people's minds completely. Otherwise, the symbol would be unable to mobilise the clan or reproduce the bonds of solidarity that keep the clan together. It would have no efficacy.

Durkheim's influence is apparent in Evans-Pritchard's work on Zande witchcraft but the latter also goes beyond Durkheim. As I have already suggested, for Evans-Pritchard, witchcraft not only expresses and reproduces the moral values of Zande society; it is also the way in which the Zande explain misfortune. By assigning this double role to witchcraft, Evans-Pritchard posits a social unconscious along Durkheimian lines and, as will become apparent below, a cultural unconscious as well. Having said that, I should point out that Evans-Pritchard's treatment of both explanations of witchcraft does much to downplay the implication that the Azande are oblivious to its true meaning and significance. It is important to note, for instance, that unlike Durkheim, Evans-Pritchard avoids the term 'symbol' altogether and employs the term 'idiom' instead: witchcraft is 'the idiom in which the Azande speak about [misfortune]' (1976: 19) or again, 'it is in the idiom of witchcraft that Azande express moral rules' (1976: 51). Unlike a symbol, which is always something other than what it appears to be, an idiom is only idiosyncratic speech, a particular way of saying something. If witchcraft is an idiom rather than a symbol, the difference between 'us' and 'them' in speaking about misfortune becomes one of mere linguistic convention. When we wish to explain why a certain granary collapsed when certain people were sitting underneath it, we say that it was an 'accident'. The Azande say that it was 'witchcraft'.

That Evans-Pritchard tries to deal with witchcraft in this way is of course understandable. Unlike Durkheim, who was caught up in the Eurocentric ideology of the nineteenth century and would not hesitate to call natives 'rudimentary intelligences', Evans-Pritchard was striving to redeem them. His aim was to show that the Zande were neither mystical nor pre-logical, but rational people like us. Nonetheless, his salvation intent notwithstanding, he was in the end unable to avoid positing a Zande social unconscious. Having discussed how the Azande use witchcraft in their everyday lives, he proceeds 'in a more objective manner' (1976: 33) to explain how witchcraft uses them – that is, how witchcraft acts to discourage their 'uncharitable impulses' (1976: 54), to eliminate friction among them, to maintain and reproduce the social order. For this to be possible at all, however, witchcraft cannot be an 'idiom' – a mere linguistic convention – as Evans-Pritchard argues; it must be backed up by supernatural sanctions. In other words, it must be understood not the way the ethnographer explains it but the way the Zande understand it – as a mysterious force beyond their control.

In a similar vein, Evans-Pritchard posits a Zande cultural unconscious. Even though he treats witchcraft 'as a mode of thought' (1976: 33) and therefore as a reflective process, in his account it emerges as the kind of thought that does not, and cannot think itself, at least not without destroying itself in the process; it emerges, in other words, as something that must remain unconscious of its truth. Evans-Pritchard tries to deny this. The Zande, he argues, explain witchcraft the way they do for two rather circumstantial reasons. First – and in this he follows Durkheim – 'the subject is too general and indeterminate, both too vague and too immense, to be described concisely' (1976: 23). Second, the Azande are not interested in such theoretical descriptions: 'they experience feelings about witchcraft rather than ideas. ... Their response is action and not analysis.' Being more interested in practice, 'the Zande actualizes these beliefs rather than intellectualizes them' (1976: 31). Otherwise, Evans-Pritchard (1976: 23) points out, 'their philosophy [of witchcraft] is explicit', even if 'not formally stated as a doctrine'. Had not the subject been so broad and fuzzy, and had the Azande developed the habit of 'intellectualizing' their practices, they would probably be able to say: '"I believe in natural causation but I do not think that that fully explains coincidences, and it seems to me that the theory of witchcraft offers a satisfactory explanation of them"' (1976: 23). The Zande do not say this of course, but Evans-Pritchard's argument is that they could articulate their belief in witchcraft in this way under the circumstances just described.

Evans-Pritchard's claim raises an important question the implications of which he hardly considers. If the Zande rationalised witchcraft the way in which Evans-Pritchard did, would it remain a meaningful way of making arbitrary events meaningful? Would there be any need for the Azande to employ witchcraft as an explanation of misfortune over and above empirical causation? In short, would witchcraft survive Evans-Pritchard's disenchanting analysis? This is highly unlikely. If the Azande were persuaded to adopt Evans-Pritchard's interpretation, they would lose faith in it. Best proof of this is what happened to Evans-Pritchard himself who was a practising Catholic. As Morris (1987: 72) points out, his studies of the Azande and the Nuer 'had precisely the effect he viewed with alarm', namely, to 'render theistic beliefs untenable'. This is an ironic consequence perhaps, but certainly instructive. By analysing the Zande cultural unconscious, Evans-Pritchard became aware of his own; by disenchanting the natives' faith, he became disenchanted with, and lost his own Catholic faith. Evans-Pritchard's personal experience confirms what he tries so hard to deny about the Zande: that witchcraft is one of those modes of thought that cannot think itself without destroying itself in the process. Its truth must remain unconscious.

And so the story of the native unconscious – the sociocultural unthought that ethnographers think out and analyse while natives only bear its silent load – continues into the 1960s in the work of Claude Lévi-Strauss and Mary Douglas. Both posit this unconscious explicitly, the latter rather reluctantly perhaps, the former quite emphatically. To turn to Lévi-Strauss first, his work on mythology provides the clearest illustration of his version of the native unconscious. Not that it is only native myths that are based on the 'unconscious structures' of the human mind, but, as he points out in *The Raw and the Cooked*, 'mythology, more than anything else, makes it possible to illustrate such objectified thought' (1969: 11). What Lévi-Strauss wants to illustrate about this thought is 'not how men think in myths, but how myths operate in men's minds without their being aware of the fact' (1969: 12), not how 'men' use myths, but how myths use 'men' instead. There is, then, something fundamental about native mythology that the natives themselves do not know; and it is this that Lévi-Strauss proposes to think out and analyse for them. The natives themselves must remain the passive instrument through which myth – now an objectified entity – operates in its mysterious ways. This is not to say that, for Lévi-Strauss, natives are inherently incapable of coming to terms with the truth of their myths – the truth, that is, which Lévi-Strauss posits. As he points out, in principle they can, but there are important reasons that prevent them from actualising this possibility.

For Lévi-Strauss, pretty much like Durkheim and Evans-Pritchard before him, one of these reasons is the practical nature of native life, the fact the natives are in the business of living rather than in the business of reflecting about life. Unlike his predecessors, however, Lévi-Strauss appears to be aware that practical considerations are not sufficient by themselves to account for the native unconscious. Thus, even if implicitly and almost as an afterthought, he also raises the question of the myths' symbolic efficacy. It may be worthwhile to quote this passage at some length.

> Although the possibility cannot be excluded that the speakers who create and transmit myths may become aware of their structure and mode of operation, this cannot occur as a normal thing, but only partially and intermittently. It is the same with myths as with language: the individual who conscientiously applied phonological and grammatical laws in his speech, supposing he possessed the necessary knowledge and virtuosity to do so, would nevertheless lose the thread of his ideas almost immediately. In the same way the *practice* and the *use* of mythological thought demand that its properties remain hidden: otherwise the subject would find himself in the position of the mythologist who cannot *believe* in myths because it is his task to take them to pieces. (1969: 11–12; my emphases)

The comparison that Lévi-Strauss makes between language and myth does not work very well and in fact obfuscates the question of belief that he also raises. He is certainly right in pointing out that it would be impractical to apply consciously structural rules to either speech or the narration of myth. But there is also a fundamental difference between the two cases. The speakers of any language would hardly become disenchanted with it even if they gained access to its unconscious rules, but the narrators of myths would most certainly lose faith in them. As a symbolic system, language has to do with semantic meaning, but myth is related in addition to existential meaning and the metaphysical realm. The truth of myths, then, must remain hidden from the native eyes but this is not only because of the practical limits that the narration of myth imposes. It is also because, as Lévi-Strauss is clearly aware, like the 'mythologist', natives would no longer believe in them. Even on this point, Lévi-Strauss's argument is slightly misleading. It is not because they make it their task to take myths apart that mythologists do not believe in them. It would be more accurate to say that they decide to take them apart because they have no faith in them to begin with. For mythologists like Lévi-Strauss, myths are not sacred histories;[4] they are imaginary tales. It is only after they have been disenchanted that myths can become an object of reflection and analysis. The point, in any case, is that when myths become disenchanted, they can no longer 'operate in men's minds'. Natives might still wish to narrate them, but they would do so the same way in which 'we' narrate poetry or read fiction.

What is it about myths, then, that natives do not know? The truth of any myth, Lévi-Strauss points out, is not what the myth says but what it does. Take, for example, the Bororo myth about a young man who raped his mother (1969: 35–7). It tells of the father's attempts to avenge himself by sending the son on dangerous missions, about the help that the young man receives from his grandmother, his adventures in the world of the souls and his encounter with various animals. And in the end, the myth tells about how the son returns to the village and kills his father. Lévi-Strauss relates this story to several similar stories from neighbouring communities and, to simplify his complex and exhaustive analysis, argues that the myth explains the origin of the cooking of food. What is significant about this is that in these native communities cooking is viewed as a form of mediation between such radical oppositions as 'heaven and earth, life and death, nature and society' (1969: 65). Thus, by means of the notion of cooking, natives explain the transition from nature to culture (from the raw to the cooked); they think of death as the reverse of the overcooked (or burned), that is, as the rotten; or they prevent the catastrophic coming together of the sun and the earth by replicating the union in a harmless way – the cooking fire. The Bororo myth, then, like all myths, is a cultural tool placed at the service of logic. It resolves logical contradictions at the symbolic level, which is to say, by replacing an original, radical opposition with one that has room for a middle term. It is this function of myths to which the natives who create and narrate them are oblivious. And it is this truth that must remain hidden from their eyes – a cultural unconscious in its own right – if myths are to have any symbolic efficacy and continue to operate as tools for the resolution of problems of logic.

To turn to Mary Douglas and her work on pollution and taboo, much like Evans-Pritchard himself, she posits both a social and a cultural unconscious. In the former case, she follows Durkheim quite closely; in the latter, she draws on Victor Turner's work on the effectiveness of symbols as well as on Lévi-Strauss's early work on the same topic. As in the case of all the authors examined so far, Douglas attributes the native unconscious to the needs of practice. The burning issues in 'primitive cultures' (as well as 'ours'), according to Douglas (1966: 91), are practical. They are about 'how to organise other people and oneself in relation to them; how to control turbulent youth, how to soothe disgruntled neighbours, how to gain one's rights, how to prevent usurpation of authority, or how to justify it'. We have our own way of dealing with such problems, 'primitive' societies have theirs. 'To serve these practical ends all kinds of beliefs in the omniscience and omnipotence of the environment are called into play' – beliefs, that is, 'about automatic punishment, destiny, ghostly vengeance and witchcraft'. The point is that, because these beliefs are constituted as instruments for practical use, because they develop as 'appendage[s] of other social institutions', they are 'rarely ... an object of contemplation and speculation'. Hence, Douglas goes on to explain, 'to this extent the primitive culture must be taken to be *unaware* of itself, *unconscious* of its own conditions' (1966: 91; my emphases).

In true Durkheimian fashion, then, Douglas posits a social unconscious. Practical social life cannot wait for 'scientific' answers to its problems. It must invent answers here and now without being particularly concerned about intellectual consistency and logic. If what is invented is to operate as an 'automatic' mechanism for the resolution of social problems, however, it must be placed beyond questioning. People must forget that it is they who invest things and themselves with cosmic powers; they must treat these powers as autonomous agents that operate outside human control. Thus, to return to the example of the Mae Enga of New Guinea, the men of this tribe must truly believe that menstrual blood depletes their strength, since in their case, there are 'no softening legal fictions [to] intervene [and] protect the freedom of the sexes' (Douglas 1966: 146). In short, if the symbolic, meta-physical system that regulates the social structure is to be effective, it must be misunderstood and misrecognised. Douglas articulates this quite clearly in her discussion of magic and ritual where, as I have already suggested, she also posits a native cultural unconscious.

In this discussion, Douglas raises the question of the efficacy of magical practices. She refers the reader to Mauss's comparison between magic and false currency and argues that on this point, Mauss was wrong.

Money can only perform its role of intensifying economic interaction if the public has faith in it. If faith is shaken, the currency is useless. So too with ritual; its symbols can only have effect so long as they command confidence. ... There is no false money except by contrast with another currency which has more total acceptability. So primitive ritual is like good money, not false money, so long as it commands assent. (1966: 69)

Like money, then, magic presupposes belief. If, however, magic does not work miracles – as ethnographers are well aware and natives are not – the question arises as to 'what kind of effectiveness is generated by the power of its symbols' (1966: 70). To answer this question, Douglas quotes approvingly Victor Turner and Lévi-Strauss. In Turner's analysis, the symbols that the shaman manipulates are shown to effect the cure of a sick man by bringing out into the open his grudges against his fellow villagers and the grudges of his fellow villagers against him. In Lévi-Strauss's analysis, the shaman cures a sick women by forcing her to focus on what went wrong during her labour. What is involved in both cases, according to the ethnographers, is rational-isation of problematic situations. In other words, symbols are effective precisely because they operate as instruments of explanation.

Douglas (1966: 72) concludes her discussion accordingly, that is, by pointing out that 'so far from being meaningless, it is primitive magic which gives meaning to existence'. But magic can give meaning to existence, and hence cure the patients, only because all the actors involved have faith in the shaman's supernatural powers. As Turner points out, 'nothing less than ritual sanctions ... and belief in the doctor's mystical powers could bring about' the conditions necessary for cure. And Lévi-Strauss concurs: 'It is of no importance that the mythology of the Shaman does not correspond to objective reality: the patient believes in it', and this is what really counts.[5] Thus, what the natives do not know and must not become aware of, is that in reality, the shaman possesses no cosmic powers at all, and that the patients get well only because they begin to come to terms with their particular predicaments.

The foregoing discussion leads inevitably to Clifford Geertz, perhaps the most articulate exponent of culturalism. Unlike Lévi-Strauss and Mary Douglas who posit a cultural unconscious explicitly, Geertz does not raise the issue directly, at least, not in his influential essay on religion. In order to flesh out the cultural unconscious in Geertz's work, then, it is necessary to re-state in broad outline his culture theory and draw a significant distinction that he does not draw – the distinction between semantic and existential meaning. Culture, according to Geertz, is a system of symbols that have meaning. It is a source of information, but an extrinsic one, since we create meaning and deposit it in things outside ourselves, namely, symbols. This is in contrast to intrinsic sources of information, what already exists in our genetic make-up in the form of instincts. Every system of information that we create is cultural and this applies as much to religion as to science or art, even though not all cultural systems are of one piece. Take science and religion, for instance. The former, according to Geertz (1973b: 112), is characterised by 'institutionalized skepticism'; it detaches itself from the world and dissolves its 'givenness' – the certainties about the world – 'into a swirl of probabilistic hypothesis'. Religion, on the other hand, is committed to certainty, to 'wider, nonhypothetical truths', and, insofar as it questions the world, it does so for the sake of these truths rather than for the sake of scepticism. Nonetheless, these differences aside, both religion and science are products of the human mind and hence both provide meaningful information about the world. In short, both are cultural systems.

There is much to be said about the differences between science and religion that Geertz posits, but here I am concerned with those differences that he does not recognise. There is certainly no objection in saying that both are cultural systems as long as one bears in mind that religious symbols are not of the same order as the symbols that science or common sense use. It is one thing to use symbols that explain what a dam is and how it is to be built,[6] and quite another to use symbols that explain why there is injustice and suffering in the world. The meaning of the former is purely semantic, that of the latter is, in addition, existential and metaphysical.

This distinction is significant because, as I have already suggested in the discussion on Evans-Pritchard, Lévi-Strauss and Mary Douglas, semantic symbols do not lose their efficacy, even when their underlying structure becomes known to the users. The efficacy of existential symbols, on the other hand, depends entirely on this structure remaining hidden from the user's eyes. The construction engineer who uses a design to build a dam and becomes aware that this design is nothing more than 'a model of and a model for reality' (Geertz 1973b: 93) does not lose faith in the project; nor does the speaker of a language who finds out that words are arbitrary constructs lose faith in the language's ability to signify. By contrast, the Zande who makes a distinction between witchcraft as a means of explaining misfortune and witchcraft as a bodily substance with malicious intent would lose faith in it before long. If religious symbols explain arbitrary and absurd events and thereby make the world meaningful, as Geertz argues, they must never be conceptualised by the believer in this way. If they are so understood, they would cease being an effective way of making the believer's world meaningful. They would become what they are for the ethnographer – mere religious symbols. Thus, even though Geertz does not explicitly posit a cultural unconscious, he cannot do without it either. He must assume that it exists, since his entire argument about religion depends on this very assumption.

Whether they require magico-religious symbols to reproduce the social structure or a cultural order of significance and meaning, all major twentieth-century ethnological paradigms have portrayed natives to be oblivious to the true meaning and real content of their lives. If there is a conclusion to be drawn at the end of this exploration, it is a poignant but inescapable one nonetheless: magico-religious systems operate as markers of Otherness no less today than during E.B. Tylor's time. To be sure, they operate as such markers on a different plane, for different reasons and under a different guise, but these differences aside, the result is pretty much the same: native magico-religious systems are still interpreted in a way that distinguishes 'us' from natives. The division between 'us' and 'them' that the symbolic paradigms establish may no longer be between the rational and the irrational, but it is just as fundamental. It is between the conscious and the unconscious, the thought and the unthought, between those who know the truth of the world because they think and doubt and those who are oblivious to it. As I have already suggested and will argue in greater detail in the last section of this chapter, this division is about much more than just knowledge and ignorance. It is inextricably intertwined with questions of human subjectivity and moral worth, and ultimately with what it means to be a human being.

The story of the division produced by the thought and the unthought does not end with the interpretation of native life. It continues, becomes more complex and reaches its climax when ethnographers turn to take a look at their own beliefs and practices. At that point they discover what they claim to be the truth about themselves; at that same instant, they render the division between 'us' and 'them' far deeper and more intractable. Ethnographers are now twice removed from their objects of study: once because they claim to know the truth about Others, twice because they now claim to know the truth about themselves as well.

HETERODOX CONSCIOUSNESS

In the last chapter, I argued that, whatever the differences between them, the orthodox and the heterodox are united by the same basic aim, namely, to redeem Others from the calumny of cultural inferiority by demonstrating that they are essentially and fundamentally the Same as 'us'. If, as it is often suggested, one of the key characteristics of modernity is a certain humanistic universalism, the pursuit of Sameness makes heterodox discourse as modern as orthodox ethnology. It is true, of course, that contemporary ethnological universalism is of a different nature than the universalism of the Enlighten-ment. For one thing, it is more discerning and discriminating than the latter, insofar at least as it makes a distinction between cultural form and cultural substance. Contemporary anthropology celebrates difference in terms of cultural form, what in the discipline goes by the name of 'cultural diversity'. But it also celebrates, and just as much, unity in terms of substance, that is, Sameness at the level of cultural value and worth. The latter principle may not be quite the same thing as 'the psychic unity of mankind' but it is hardly any less encompassing and universal.

But beyond humanist universalism, orthodox anthropology and heterodox discourse are united by another equally fundamental modernist theme, what in the last chapter I referred to as the logic that objectifies and disenchants the world. No doubt, it is easy to criticise heterodox discourse as an anti-modernist movement, and equally easy to point to its attack on objectivity as proof, as indeed all those ethnographers who are entrenched in the positivist canon have done. But this is little more than a defensive response that helps us understand neither heterodox discourse nor modernity. Indeed, by conflating science and modernity, the positivist reaction obfuscates our understanding of both even more. Let us, then, first say that science is neither synonymous with modernity nor its cause; on the contrary, it is modernity's product. As Max Weber (1946b: 138) points out, science is only 'a fraction', even if 'the most important fraction' of a much wider orientation toward the world – an attitude of 'intellectualization and rationalization'. This attitude, which for Weber (1946b: 139) constitutes the very essence of modernity, 'means principally that there are no mysterious incalculable forces [in the world] but rather that one can, in principle, master all things by calculation. This means that the world is disenchanted'.

Heterodox discourse is armed and operates with this fundamental modernist weapon, even if it is using this weapon against itself or, at any rate, against that of which it is an integral part – anthropology. But in this process of self-cannibalisation, heterodox discourse does nothing more than be consistent with the modernist logic that inspires and directs anthropol-ogy itself. This is the logic, it may be recalled, that modernist science employed in the eighteenth and nineteenth centuries to objectify and disenchant religion. When 'science encounters the claims of the ethical postulate that the world is a God-ordained, and hence somehow *meaning-fully* and ethically oriented, cosmos', Max Weber (1946c: 350–1) reminds us, it 'pushes religion from the rational into the irrational realm'. It does so because science discovers that, far from being a benevolent universe, the world is neutral and indifferent to human concerns. Weber does not raise the question of what would happen when, sooner or later, science encountered its own enchanted presuppositions – among them the key assumption that representation operates as if it were the immaculate conception of a transcendental being and that, therefore, it can be relied upon to furnish us with the truth of the world. If science is to be consistent with its own logic, however, it has no option but to treat its own claims the same way in which it treated religion, namely, as 'fiction'. Indeed, this is exactly what that alleged arch-anti-modernist, Michel Foucault, has done in his analysis of 'the human sciences', and what other post-structuralist, deconstructive authors such a Derrida are doing in philosophy and elsewhere. This too has been the path that heterodox ethnographers followed in their own critique of anthropology – a path that makes their discourse consistently and uncompromisingly modernist.

Realisation of the consistently modernist orientation of post-structuralist discourse has been behind recent attempts in social theory, such as those by Giddens and Beck, to 'modernise modernity'. No doubt this is largely a defensive strategy, in effect an attempt to save modernity by containing the runaway effects inherent in all post-structuralist thought, something that prominent post-structuralist figures such as Foucault and Derrida have not been particularly interested in doing. But, unlike the orthodox ethnological position, it is receptive to the post-structuralist critique and, insofar as it sheds new light on both modernity and 'postmodernity', far more constructive. For Giddens and Beck, modernisation of modernity consists precisely in applying to the modernist project the same sort of logic that modernity applied to the religiously dominated universe of the previous era. The most fundamental characteristic of this logic, which these authors call 'reflexivity', is that it breaks with foundationalism and certainty of any sort – or so it is argued – whether certainty about knowledge, and hence the claims of science, or history, and hence the teleological claims of metaphysics.

Reflexivity, then, is ultimately a circular project because reflection must eventually reflect on, and doubt itself – the sort of double bind that Foucault identified in his study of the 'human sciences'. But it is nonetheless a project that must be carried out, according to the theorists of 'reflexivity', despite its obviously paradoxical nature and unsettling implications. Otherwise, modernity is in danger of lapsing into traditionalism, a situation where one type of dogmatism (reason and science) would take the place of another (religion). Here is how Giddens argues the point:

Enlightenment thought, and Western culture in general, emerged from a religious context which emphasised teleology and the achievement of God's grace. Divine providence had long been a guiding idea of Christian thought. Without these preceding orientations, the Enlightenment would scarcely have been possible in the first place. It is in no way surprising that the advocacy of unfettered reason only reshaped the ideas of the providential, rather than displacing it. One type of certainty (divine law) was replaced by another (the certainty of our senses, of empirical observation), and divine providence was replaced by providential progress ... . If, [however] the sphere of reason is wholly unfettered, no knowledge can rest upon an unquestioned foundation, because even the most firmly held notions can only be regarded as valid 'in principle' or 'until further notice'. Otherwise they would relapse into dogma and become separate from the very sphere of reason which determines what validity is in the first place. (1990: 48–9)

For Giddens, then, the essence of modernity is neither reason nor science but reflexivity – the breaking up with foundationalism and the certainty about the world that this entails. Unlike certain modernist ethnographers who fetishise both reason and science, he is perceptive enough to see in them a historically specific expression of reflexivity, one that evolved partly in reaction to religious dogmatism. In this way, Giddens co-opts and appropriates post-structuralist thought. He is able to show that post-structuralism is a thoroughly modernist project – a project that does nothing more than to apply reflexivity to itself. Hence, for Giddens, post-structuralism is not 'taking us "beyond modernity"', as the term 'postmodernity' suggests. Rather, it 'provide[s] a fuller understanding of the reflexivity inherent in modernity itself' (1990: 49). The most one could say about the present condition, according to Giddens, is that it is a period of 'high modernity' – a modernity, that is, which is modernising itself by calling into question its own foundationalist tendencies.

All this goes to show that heterodox ethnographers are far more consistent in their use of the modernist logic than the orthodox apologists of ethnological modernity. They treat science, or, to be more precise, the scientific pretensions of the discipline, the same way in which science treated religion, tradition and other foundational systems of thought. Heterodox ethnographers objectify and disenchant the discipline's scientific pretensions by reminding all those who may have forgotten that ethnological representations and everything that depends on them – science, objectivity, the truth – are things that we have invented and inserted into the world, just like any other historical construct; and that it would be sheer delusion for the ethnographer to believe otherwise, however tempting and reassuring this may be.

Heterodox ethnographers, then, have modernised ethnological modernity by bringing it face to face with what was hidden in the silent regions of the ethnographer's consciousness. In the aftermath of their critique, the discipline has no more secrets to keep from itself and can look itself straight in the eye. It now knows itself. Up until very recently it only claimed to know Others – what they are, what they do, how and why they do it. Now it claims to know itself as well – what it truly is, what it really does, exactly how and why it does it, how much it can expect from itself. Modernised ethnological modernity has now reached a new level of enlightenment and generates more light and more truth than ever before. And yet, in the midst of this auspicious conjuncture, hardly anyone has noticed that the division which ethnographers now draw between themselves and those they study has suddenly become sharper and deeper, that they now distance themselves from Others as they have never done before. Not only do ethnographers know what the natives do not know about themselves; they now know everything that can be known about their own ethnographic selves. To illustrate how this radical division is effected, I shall turn to a few examples from the heterodox literature.

To begin with, the heterodox critique of ethnological representation suggests that ethnographers are not or, at any rate, should not be as innocent as Tylor's 'primitives'. As we have seen, for Tylor (1874: 305), natives represent the childhood stage of humanity, 'the poetic stage of thought'. Their stage of development is 'poetic' because natives think and speak like poets, using metaphors, similes and other expressive, rhetorical devices; but it is also a stage of innocence because they take the imaginary worlds they construct quite literally – 'what we call poetry [is] to them real life' (Tylor 1874: 297). It would seem that, for a long time, ethnographers have been behaving more or less like Tylor's natives. For they too have been using metaphors, similes and other expressive, rhetorical devices in their accounts, and they too, naively and innocently perhaps, have been treating these accounts as objective descriptions of actual events, as 'real life' – native life. This fundamental misconception, however, cannot be allowed to persist in our midst. It has become far too embarrassing and must be stopped at once. After all, the condescending and patronising denials notwithstanding, ethnographers and natives are not the Same thing.

Ethnographers, then, have been deluding themselves for too long in a cultural universe where delusions have no place. It is time that they are told the truth, however disturbing it might be. Here is how Stephen Tyler tells it:

A post-modern ethnography is a cooperatively evolved text consisting of fragments of discourse intended to evoke in the minds of both reader and writer an emergent *fantasy of a possible world* of commonsense reality, and thus to provoke an aesthetic integration that will have a *therapeutic* effect. It is, in a word, *poetry* – not in its textual form, but in its return to the original context and function of poetry, which, by means of its performative break with everyday speech, evoked memories of the ethos of the community and thereby provoked hearers to act ethically. (1986: 125–6; my emphases)

It would seem that there is a fundamental distinction to be made between 'us' and 'them'. Unlike Tylor's innocent primitives who are unconscious of the true meaning of their myths – who are poets without realising it – ethnographers are now aware of what they truly are. They now realise that what they write is not science but poetry. Thanks to heterodox discourse, ethnographers have learned that the point in what they do is not to tell the truth about Others, but merely stories. They now know, in addition, that such stories are not merely aesthetically pleasing but also help to heal troubled subjectivities. Indeed, unlike those who may think that poetry has only aesthetic value, ethnographers are now well aware that it also has therapeutic effects. In short, not only do ethnographers now know exactly what they do. They also know exactly what they do does.

The heterodox critique of ethnological representation serves to distinguish ethnographers at the expense not only of Tylor's innocent primitive, but also of the kind of native that twentieth-century anthropology has fashioned – the symbolic type. It does so because it refuses to acknowledge that some ethnological beliefs and practices may be symbolic as well or, to be more precise, it does not tolerate their existence and seeks to disenchant them at every opportunity. In effect, the heterodox critique distances the ethnographer from the 'symbolic' kind of native because it refuses to tolerate what it perceives to be the discipline's own sociocultural unconscious. A characteristic example of this double standard has to do with the question of time reversal and becomes apparent when one contrasts what ethnographers say about natives in this respect and how they react to the possibility that their beliefs and practices may be implicated in the same sort of temporal inversion.

In many native societies, the ethnological story goes, there are certain periods, such as during ritual, when the flow of time is reversed. To use Lévi-Strauss's (1966: 237) celebrated phrase, 'historical rites bring the past into the present and the rites of mourning the present into the past'. Such practices, ethnographers explain, are symbolic. As Lévi-Strauss (1966: 236) himself points out, in the case of historical rites, natives seek to recreate 'the sacred and beneficial atmosphere of mythical times' and in this way deny the profanity of the present, while, in the case of mourning rites, their aim is to deny the finality of death. In short, rites of time reversal, pretty much like other magico-religious practices, transform arbitrary and absurd happenings into meaningful events.

This sort of explanation of time reversal is nothing more than a condescending and patronising treatment of native lives. Ethnographers themselves render it condescending and patronising because they refuse to accept that their own beliefs and practices may be implicated in the same sort of symbolic inversion of time. When ethnographers turn around to look at themselves, symbolism is put aside and an old-fashioned positivism – in many ways reminiscent of the kind advocated by Tylor himself – becomes the instrument of explanation. Ethnographers are happy to declare that native lives are symbolic but, for their own beliefs and practices, they adopt an attitude that recognises nothing other than the facts of the empirical world. This is well illustrated by, among others, the work of Johannes Fabian (1983) and the argument he developed on the uses of time in anthropology – an argument that has been adopted wholeheartedly by heterodox ethnographers themselves.[7]

As is well known, Fabian's thesis is that time in ethnological discourse is used in ways that deny Other societies 'coevalness' – by which he means the same temporal existence – and hence, by extension, cultural equality as well. This double denial is effected in various ways, according to Fabian (1983: 23), the most common being the use of 'typological time', that is, of temporal concepts like 'traditional', 'preliterate' and 'peasant' to designate native societies. Such terms, the argument continues, are not innocent. They are loaded with cultural significance, since they exist and operate in relation to their opposites – 'modern', 'literate', 'industrial' – which ethnographers use to designate themselves. By describing native societies as traditional or peasant, then, ethnographers suggest that these societies are at a stage of development which modern, industrial societies surpassed centuries ago. In effect, they suggest that native societies exist in the Western past.

For Fabian, and the heterodox ethnographers who have embraced his argument, this claim is sheer fiction – rather than a symbolic statement of some sort. As Fabian explains (1983: 71), it is fiction precisely because 'productive empirical research is possible only when researcher and researched share Time'. Such, after all, are the incontrovertible facts of the empirical world. Sheer common sense (not to say positive science) dictates that no one can take the present into the past – to conduct fieldwork – or bring the past into the present – to speak and write about what one has found. It dictates that no one can reverse the flow of time – no one, that is, except Others. But ethnographers are not like Others and therefore cannot be allowed to delude themselves in this way. If ethnological beliefs and practices are symbolic like native ritual, they must not be allowed to remain blind to their truth. They must be disenchanted and demystified so that the naked reality below the symbol, as Durkheim would say, is exposed for what it is. There is a biting irony in Fabian's argument. In the same book, unaware of his own lapse into ethnocentrism, Fabian (1983: 131–41) criticises 'symbolic anthropology' for positing a practical, economistic Self and a symbolic Other.

This, then, is the way in which heterodox discourse entrenches the division that the symbolic paradigms of the twentieth century first established – the division, that is, between the conscious and the unconscious, the thought and the unthought. If, up to now, anthropology functioned as the ethnographers' own cultural unconscious, this is no longer possible. Ethnographers are now well aware of the secret that their discipline has kept hidden for so long. And if, up to now, it was possible to say that, given this cultural unconscious, ethnographers and those they study are fundamentally similar in this respect, this is no longer possible either. There is now an unbridgeable gap separating 'us' and 'them'. Not only have ethnographers thought the natives' unthought and disenchanted native metaphysical symbols. They have now thought and disenchanted theirs as well. With this, the ethnocentric ethnological edifice is now complete and everything appears as if ethnographers, unlike natives, cannot forget the naked truth of the world, whether they are speaking about Others or about themselves; as if, and as a result of their persistent remembering of this truth, they live in a thoroughly disenchanted universe without any metaphysical illusions – whether religion, magic or immaculately conceived representations. In short, the image of the world that emerges in the aftermath of the heterodox critique is one in which Others require myths to protect themselves from the meaninglessness of the world and are thus happy in their self-induced ignorance, while ethnographers, who refuse the support of such crutches, may not be as happy but neither are they as ignorant.

Yet if this is how things appear, it is only because the story told by heterodox discourse is incomplete. It is far from being completed because heterodox ethnographers have forgotten the most important part. The heterodox story may have a beginning, a middle and an end but it lacks substance. It has nothing whatsoever to say about what makes anthropology what it is, the discipline's condition of possibility and reason for existence. Heterodox discourse tells us much about epistemology and does much to undermine the discipline's scientific pretensions but this is neither here nor there. Contrary to what both orthodox and heterodox ethnographers think, it is not science that makes anthropology. It is the axiomatic representation of Sameness, about which heterodox discourse has nothing at all to say.

Heterodox ethnographers have been more consistent than their orthodox counterparts in their use of the modernist logic that objectifies and disenchants the world. They have used it to disenchant the scientific aura which surrounded anthropology. But, despite their reflexivity, their determination to expose all ethnological secrets and to eradicate all ethnological illusions notwithstanding, they have forgotten to reflect on and talk about the best-kept ethnological secret of all. An agonistic discourse, such as this one, that plays the ethnological game of knowledge to end the ethnological game of power cannot forget to remember Sameness. If the ethnological game of knowledge is played on the basis of the modernist logic, an agonistic postcolonial discourse must be more modernist in the application of this logic than the modernists themselves. If the modernist logic is used to objectify and disenchant the things of the world, an agonistic postcolonial discourse must objectify and disenchant everything in the world of anthropology, particularly what remains hidden and unthought. If what it takes to disenchant the ethnological unthought is the objectification of Sameness, an agonistic postcolonial discourse must objectify, disenchant and demystify it. In short, an agonistic discourse must play the ethnological game to the full and to the very end. Its aim can be nothing other than to beat ethnographers at their own game – and then invite them for another round. I shall turn to the task of objectifying and demystifying Sameness in the next chapter. For now, it is necessary to address a possible objection.

It could be argued that the division between the thought and the unthought that I have been discussing is unintentional, committed as it is in the course of trying to demonstrate Sameness. It was necessary for Evans-Pritchard to explain witchcraft in symbolic terms because the alternative would have been endorsement of Lévy-Bruhl's thesis and hence of the division of the world between the logical and the pre-logical. And, it could also be pointed out, it was necessary for heterodox ethnographers to expose ethnological discourse as poetry and time reversal in ethnological practice as fiction because the alternative would have been nothing less than tolerating all sorts of divisions between 'us' and 'them' that orthodox anthropology has effected in the course of the last 150 years. All this is true, no doubt, but this is exactly the point and the paradox that the present discourse is trying to bring into the open and highlight: ethnographers divide the world despite themselves – not because they wish to divide it but because they strive to unite it.

The division between the thought and the unthought, then, is without doubt an unintended consequence of the ethnological endeavour. But lack of intention makes this division neither less real nor less pernicious. To suggest, on the one hand, that natives require myths to protect themselves from the meaninglessness of the world and, on the other, that ethnographers refuse such sheltering illusions is plainly ethnocentric. Indeed, ethnographers themselves would be the first to point this out. Yet to recognise this as an ethnocentric claim already presupposes a system of moral evaluation in which the act of refusing comforting but false images of the world is invested with higher value than the act of embracing them. It presupposes a certain ontology of the self in which individuals are expected to struggle for the truth, irrespective of the sacrifices that might be involved in this struggle. Had not this been the case, the division between the thought and the unthought would be colourless and neutral – certainly not ethnocentric – and ethnological sensibilities would not be offended. Indeed, it would hardly be a relevant division at all. In the last analysis, therefore, it makes little difference if the division between the thought and the unthought that ethnographers effect is unintentional. What is important is that it is effected in a wider cultural universe in which disenchantment and demystification or, to be more precise, the attitude responsible for them, is invested with superior moral value. And that ethnographers, whether they are prepared to admit it or not, share the assumptions of this cultural universe as much as anyone else.

THE 'HEROISATION' OF THE THINKING SUBJECT

In 1784 Kant published a short essay in which he raised the question as to what Enlightenment is about. From the ethnological point of view this otherwise obscure piece of work is highly significant; in the course of answering this question, Kant establishes the ground on which the West imagines itself. More specifically, in this essay he outlines the ontology of the modern self and discusses the means by which it can be achieved. For Kant, as for virtually all Enlightenment and post-Enlightenment thinkers, to be is to be free and to be free is to think for oneself. The modern subject can only be a thinking subject because it is only by thinking for oneself and by doubting what has already been established and institutionalised – 'the received wisdom' – that one can become an autonomous individual. Enlightenment, Kant points out, is:

man's emergence from his self-incurred immaturity. *Immaturity* is the inability to use one's own understanding without the guidance of another. This immaturity is *self-incurred* if its cause is not lack of understanding, but lack of resolution and courage to use it without the guidance of another. The motto of enlightenment is therefore: *Sapere aude*! Have courage to use your *own* understanding! (1970a [1784]: 54; emphases in the original)

Let us first note that Kant's call for enlightenment entails a certain heroic attitude. To become enlightened, and hence a 'mature' human being, one needs 'resolution' and 'courage', even 'audacity' – *sapere aude* (have the audacity to be wise). These heroic attributes are called for because to use one's 'own understanding', to think for oneself, means to refuse the 'dogmas and the formulas' (1970a: 54) in one's culture. In effect, it means that one must be prepared to swim against the current and if necessary, to stand completely alone. All 'men' are capable of thinking for themselves, according to Kant, since all are endowed with reason. Not all, however, are industrious or daring enough to do so; 'laziness and cowardice are the reasons why such a large proportion of men, even when nature has long emancipated them from alien guidance ... nevertheless gladly remain immature for life' (1970a: 54).

To think for oneself, then, is both easy and difficult. It is easy because everyone possesses the rational faculties to think, but it is also difficult because it often means venturing by oneself on to unfamiliar ground. Because it takes courage to do so, the world is full of unenlightened, 'immature' people – people, that is, who are wholly dependent on others. For Kant, a life of dependency and domination is clearly not fit for human beings. Speaking of 'the guardians', for example, those who take it upon themselves to lead others through life, he depicts the following picture:

Having first infatuated their domesticated animals, and carefully prevented the docile creatures from daring to take a single step without the leading-strings to which they are tied, they next show them the danger which threatens them if they try to walk unaided. (1970a: 54)

The metaphors that Kant employs to speak about those who do not dare think for themselves may sound harsh to contemporary ears. The rhetoric aside, however, the message is surely familiar and rings true. To be on the leash is something that the modern liberal self recognises as incompatible with human dignity.

There are three important points to note about Kant's essay. First, it is concerned with individual autonomy; second, it argues that this can be achieved only by means of free thinking, the use of one's own understanding, so that for Kant individual autonomy and reflection become inseparable; and third, it claims that freedom is reserved for those who have courage, those who venture beyond the boundaries of the given and dare think new thoughts. The essay, then, establishes vital links between individual autonomy, thinking and doubting and a certain heroic attitude that characterises those who think the unthought. In what follows, I locate these three themes in the work of several prominent authors and contrast the culture of the heroic, thinking and hence autonomous subject with the way in which ethnographers have been interpreting native lives. Before I turn to this task however, it may be useful to make a brief reference to the sociological and psychological versions of Kant's argument – useful as a reminder, if one is needed, of the extent to which this way of looking at the world permeates Western thought.

For Kant, and for the authors whose work I shall examine below, the stake in not thinking for oneself is dependence on others. But human lives are not only subject to other individuals; they are also subject to impersonal forces that exist and operate beyond the individual's knowledge and control. In the history of the Western intellectual tradition, this idea branches off into two directions, one social, the other psychological. The former is the direction taken by the sociological school of thought and the kind of inquiry that runs from Marx and Durkheim to Giddens and Bourdieu. As is well known, the essence of the argument developed by this school of thought is that life is determined (or shaped, or conditioned) by societal forces – whether the infrastructure, social facts or social conditions internalised and operating as 'habitus'; and that freedom becomes possible only when these forces are mastered and brought under control. Hence the distinction that is often drawn between societies that make their own history and are masters of their destiny and societies that are made by history instead. The second direction has been developed by Freud and informs the psychological tradition. The forces to be mastered here are psychic – repressed desires and traumatic experiences buried deep in the unconscious that drive individuals to behave in ways which they themselves often find problematic and unacceptable. Freedom in this case consists of freedom from compulsive behaviour which is achieved when the neurotic comes to terms with what has been repressed. In both cases, then, there is a certain unthought to be thought out, an unconscious – whether social or psychic – that blocks the road to freedom. Here too, the autonomous subject can only be a daring, thinking subject.

But to return to Kant, his call for 'maturity' and the rejection of 'dogmas and formulas' must have found fertile ground since, a century later, prominent thinkers such as Schiller and Max Weber were able to declare with confidence that the Western world had become 'disenchanted'. Religious dogmas, in particular, are no longer embraced with the same sort of blind trust as in previous centuries, nor are the 'guardians' of the flock as powerful. It would appear that most people have found the courage they lacked for so long to break the fetters of ignorance that kept them bound to outside forces, whether this-worldly or otherwise. Not that 'maturity' is the sort of unmitigated blessing that Kant had imagined. Indeed, there is a certain price to be paid for the newly acquired freedom, a price that some people find far too high. In his polemical essay 'Science as a vocation', Max Weber discusses Tolstoy's rejection of enlightened modernity and criticises him for doing so. Weber acknowledges that living in a disenchanted world is not always easy, but he has no doubt either that the freedom which disenchantment makes possible is preferable to the conditions of existence in a religiously dominated universe.

For Tolstoy, Weber points out, science makes death, and therefore life itself, meaningless. In earlier times, before the advent of modernity, life gave people everything it had to offer so that they lived their lives in full and were ready to go when the time came. With the rise of science, however, what the world has to offer always extends beyond the individual's life span, so that finite human lives are now caught up in the infinite march of progress and inevitably remain unfulfilled. Under such circumstances, death has no meaning. It can no longer be considered as the natural closing of the life cycle, but appears instead as an abrupt and untimely end. Weber (1946b: 155) acknowledges that this sort of disenchantment with life and death is indeed 'the fate of our times'. But it is a fate nonetheless that he, unlike Tolstoy, is prepared to confront and grapple with.

To the person who cannot bear the fate of the times like a *man*, one must say: may he rather return silently, without the usual publicity build-up of renegades, but simply and plainly. The arms of the old churches are opened widely and compassionately for him. After all, they do not make it hard for him. One way or another he has to bring his 'intellectual sacrifice' – that is inevitable. (1946b: 155; my emphasis)

Life in a disenchanted world, then, is not easy. Having seen the light and truth, many people discover that it is painful to bear its blinding intensity. As Weber suggests, they lack the courage and determination to confront, and come to terms with what the truth reveals – a world indifferent to human concerns and hopes, an essentially arbitrary and meaningless world. Such people long for the sheltering presence of religious myths, and some, like Tolstoy, succumb in the end and embrace them. The cost involved in this surrender, however, Weber points out, is enormous. It is certainly much higher than that paid by those who persist in bearing the fate of the times. People like Tolstoy who cannot live without comforting illusions, must sacrifice their autonomy and freedom.

Let us, then, note in Weber the same sort of heroic attitude that one finds advocated in Kant's essay – an attitude underscored by Weber's masculinist vocabulary. Men are either courageous and brave or they are no men at all. Hence, any man worthy of the name should be able to bear the fate of the times. Let us also note that the stakes involved in Weber's essay are the same as in Kant's – individual autonomy and freedom. Kant encourages individuals to become autonomous subjects by daring to use their own understanding. Weber encourages them to remain autonomous subjects by summoning up the necessary courage to grapple with what free-thinking has brought about – the realisation that this is an indifferent and meaningless world.

The rhetoric of the intrepid free-thinker and destroyer of comforting myths finds its most articulate proponent in the influential figure of Martin Heidegger. Like Nietzsche before him, Heidegger was a scholar of the '*nihil*'. It should not be assumed, however, that this 'nothing' is the purely negative and nihilistic. On the contrary, for Heidegger, it is what makes everything possible.

Only because the nothing [becomes] manifest ... can the total strangeness of beings overwhelm us. Only when the strangeness of things oppresses us does it arouse and evoke wonder. Only on the ground of wonder – the revelation of the nothing – does the 'why?' loom before us. Only because the 'why' is possible as such can we inquire into grounds, and ground them. Only because we can inquire and ground is the destiny of our existence placed in [our] hands. (Heidegger 1977a: 109)

Without the 'nothing', then, there would be nothing new, only the 'givenness' of the world, as Geertz would say, in its stagnant solidity. Nor would it be possible for us to constitute the world in the way we see fit and act as its ground. On the contrary, without reflection on the 'nothing', the world would constitute and ground us instead, keep us chained to what it has already made of itself.

Important though it may be, reflection, as Heidegger understands, is hardly an easy task. As he points out, reflection is 'the courage to make the truth of our own presuppositions ... the things that most deserve to be called in question' (1977b: 116). As such, Heidegger (1977b: 137) goes on to explain, it 'is not necessarily for all, nor is it to be accomplished or even found bearable by everyone'. Indeed, reflection in general and on the 'nothing' in particular is to be accomplished only by those who 'are basically daring' (1977a: 106). One must be daring because the 'nothing' can only be revealed by anxiety, that 'altogether unsettling experience of ... hovering where there is nothing to hold onto' (1977a: 101). It takes courage and determination, then, to enter into this state of angst and face the 'nothing' and not many ordinary mortals are willing or even capable of doing such a thing. Encountering the 'nothing' means standing at the edge of the abyss – a non-place where no shelters or safety nets exist, nothing that one can turn to for protection. At this non-place 'the totality of relevance discovered within the world of things ... collapses [and] the world [acquires] the character of complete insignificance' (Heidegger 1996 [1926]: 174). At the non-place of the 'nothing', one comes face to face with the most fundamental truth of the world, namely, that one is 'thrown' into life and therefore already inevitably towards one's death, that one exists for no reason and serves no ultimate purpose. In short, one comes face to face with the utter absurdity and mean-inglessness of life.

Reflection on the 'nothing' may be difficult but it is the source of all authentic human existence – of autonomy and freedom. Most people, Heidegger (1996: 120) argues, spend their lives in a state of 'dependency and inauthenticity'. They busy themselves in the affairs of the world and do their best to avoid anxiety, to forget that in the face of which, above anything else, one is anxious – death. Indeed, there is a 'constant tranquilization about death' in everyday life, according to Heidegger (1996: 235), 'a constant flight from death'. Anticipation of death, on the other hand, reveals to the individual human being:

its lostness in the they-self, and brings it face to face with the possibility to be itself, primarily unsupported by concern taking care of things ... in passionate anxious *freedom toward death* which is free of the illusions of the they, factical, and certain of itself. (Heidegger 1996: 245)

The individual, then, is hopelessly dependent on the 'they', that is, on the illusions of one's society and culture, its everyday concerns and current mythologies. As long as one is a 'they-self', however, tranquillised and forgetful of the truth of the world – of its nothingness – one cannot be free. Freedom consists of anticipating death, of coming face to face with the predicament of the human condition and never losing sight of it. Freedom becomes possible only when the individual refuses all the crutches and false supports that ordinary life has to offer.

Heidegger's rhetoric is formidable, and his posture in the face of death verges on the dramatic. But, however overblown and exaggerated, his views are hardly any different from those encountered in Kant and Max Weber. Above all, Heidegger's message is a call for courage – the courage necessary to reflect freely on whatever exists beyond the boundaries of one's time, society and culture, which may the nothing; to stand alone without the support of, and hence without being dependent on others, even if by doing so one encounters no one and comes face to face with nothing; to plot one's trajectory through life consciously and knowingly, even if it may mean keeping in constant view the end of the trajectory, which is nothing. In short, it is a call for the courage necessary to think the unthought, whatever the costs involved, because it is only by thinking the unthought that one can become an authentic self, an autonomous subjectivity.

The three themes encountered in Kant, Weber and Heidegger – the themes of heroism, reflection and freedom – surface again in an essay by Michel Foucault (1984) that is itself entitled 'What is Enlightenment?' Foucault begins with a commentary on Kant's original essay and then focuses on what he finds novel and significant about it. Kant's essay is important, according to Foucault, because it combines two things previously kept apart. First, the essay is a reflection on the conditions of Kant's age and second, it appears to have acted as a spur for Kant's various critiques. In the essay, Kant stresses the need for the universal use of reason; in his critiques, he sets out to establish the conditions for the legitimate use of reason. In this combination – reflecting on one's era and assuming a certain 'philosophical task' related to the needs of that era – Foucault (1984: 38) discerns what he calls 'the attitude of modernity'. Thinking of modernity as an attitude, he points out, does away with the need to distinguish 'the "modern era" from the "premodern" or "postmodern"' and opens up the possibility of exploring something far more useful: 'how the attitude of modernity, ever since its formation, has found itself struggling with attitudes of "countermodernity"' (1984: 39). Foucault feels himself to be an heir to 'the attitude of modernity' but at the same time, he sharply differentiates himself from Kant. Reflecting on the conditions of *our* era, he points out, it becomes apparent that our task is no longer to set the limits that reason should avoid transgressing. This was done by Kant in the eighteenth century, and Foucault (1984: 50) is prepared to acknowledge that Kant's work 'has not been without its importance or effectiveness during the last two centuries'. But the task today is something different, in fact, quite the reverse. It is to 'experiment with the possibility of going beyond [these limits]'.

To explain more fully what he means by 'the attitude of modernity', Foucault turns to Baudelaire. For the latter, modernity is not simply a question of being aware of the movement of time, of endorsing change and a break with tradition, of valorising the present and what is new. This is something that fashion does also, but modernity is different from fashion. Modernity entails a certain relation to the present and to oneself which Baudelaire considers 'heroic'. Indeed, as Foucault (1984: 40) points out, modernity 'is the will to "heroize" the present'. Foucault (1984: 41) interprets this 'heroisation' as the 'difficult interplay between the truth of what is real and the exercise of freedom'. It is a difficult interplay because its goal is the transformation of what is real in such a way as to render the modern subject autonomous and free. 'For the attitude of modernity', Foucault (1984: 41) points out, 'the high value of the present is indissociable [sic] from a desperate eagerness to imagine it ... otherwise than it is, and to transform it not by destroying it but by grasping it in what it is.' The interplay between reality and freedom – the interrogation of reality that yields freedom – applies as much to the world as to the self. The modern subject not only seeks to grasp the world, but also takes itself as an 'object of a complex and difficult elaboration' (1984: 41). Modernity not only compels the modern subject to define the world differently from how it is, but also, at the same time, 'to face the task of producing himself' (1984: 42).

The way in which Foucault, following Baudelaire, imagines the transformation of the present – of the world and of the self – is significant and I shall return to it shortly. Let me first say that at this point in the essay, Foucault takes stock of his analysis and suggests that what we should retain from the Enlightenment is not its doctrinal elements, its universalism, for example, or emphasis on reason. It should be rather its attitude, the heroic attitude of modernity – '[the] philosophical ethos that could be described as a permanent critique of our historical era' (1984: 42). On the basis of the modern attitude, Foucault points out, it should be possible to identify those aspects of the Enlightenment that prevent us from attaining our goal and discard them – our goal being none other than 'the constitution of ourselves as autonomous subjects' (1984: 43). Foucault continues with suggestions as to how the 'permanent critique' of ourselves should be conducted, but enough has been said about his essay to allow a comparison with Kant, Weber and Heidegger.

Let us, then, note the obvious points of convergence among all four writers. The first point is the goal that these thinkers ascribe to modernity, namely, the constitution of the authentic individual – the autonomous subject. The second point of agreement relates to the mechanism by which autonomous subjectivity can be achieved, which is none other than painstaking reflection on the world and on the self by the subject itself. Let us also note an apparent – but only apparent – difference between Foucault and the other three writers. Unlike Kant, Weber and Heidegger, who speak of the need for the modern individual subject to be courageous and daring, Foucault locates this heroic attitude in what appears to be a non-personal domain – 'the present'. A closer look at Foucault's account of what should be done with the world and the self, however, shows that it is not the present as such that modernity heroises. It is, rather, the thinking subject that is expected to transform it. In modernity, as opposed to 'countermodernity', the thinking subject undertakes the monumental task of reinventing both the world and itself. It must rethink and redefine the world and itself – 'imagine it otherwise than it is' – *for itself*, which means that it must contest and replace pre-existing definitions of both. By reinventing the world and itself in this way – by means of words, and hence symbolically – the modern subject becomes autonomous. Being autonomous in this sense means being the subject that is subject to itself and to no one else, since by definition the world in which this subject now lives is its own creation and object rather than the creation of someone else. If there is anything heroic about the present, then, it is the thinking subject that undertakes the Herculean task of making the world afresh and then supporting this world in its entirety by itself, a subject that aspires to become nothing less than the Subject – the re-Creator of the world.

Foucault brings me to the end of this brief exploration of Western conceptions of the modern self – conceptions, that is, about how the self should relate to itself and the world at large. I do not pretend that this is anything other than a sketch, a broad outline of an undoubtedly multi-faceted and complex theme. I am keenly aware, for instance, that there are important Western thinkers whose views are diametrically opposed to the ones I have been discussing.[8] My aim, however, has been neither to make a comprehensive survey nor an in-depth analysis of Western notions of subjectivity – both formidable tasks and quite beyond my competence. Rather, I have tried to identify the key elements of what I take to be the dominant paradigm – dominant insofar as these elements about what the modern individual is (or should be) are employed in the construction of several well-known, institutionalised and consequential distinctions: a historical and, no doubt, ideological distinction between modernity and what preceded it – the Middle, or more tellingly, Dark Ages; a social distinction between those who are closer to culture and those closer to nature – men and women respectively being the example that most readily comes to mind;[9] and the geopolitical, cultural distinction between the West and the Other, whether this is drawn inadvertently and against one's intentions, as in the ethnographer's case, or because one's aim is to distinguish the West at the expense of the Other.

To juxtapose explicitly the determination of the thinking subject to think the unthought with the almost automatic (as Evans-Pritchard describes it, at any rate) Zande recourse to witchcraft, with any 'Azande' of the world and any kind of 'witchcraft', will perhaps appear disingenuous – a cheap rhetorical strategy. And yet, as I have already argued, this juxtaposition and the division between 'us' and 'them' that it effects already takes place whenever magico-religious beliefs and practices are explained as machines for the production of meaning. They are both effected every time the patronising argument is made that Others require myths to protect themselves from the intrinsic meaninglessness of the world. Ethnographers are being condescending and patronising because they themselves no longer believe in such myths and call for an end to those in which they had faith until recently; because they recognise the value in contesting the myths of one's society and culture; and because they have been taught to believe that it is only by contesting such myths that one becomes an autonomous subject. Ethnographers do not need to make an explicit juxtaposition between the thinking subject and the 'Azande' of the world. Their discourse is *predisposed* to divide the world between the thought and the unthought – which is a division between superior and inferior humanity – because ethnographers too valorise and 'heroise' the thinking subject. They do so because they are part of a culture that does.

One may object to this claim by pointing out that this sort of valorisation – this virtual deification of the thinking subject – is effected only by certain 'pure' and elevated thinkers, such as the ones that I have been discussing; or, at any rate, that ethnographers themselves are pragmatic creatures doing fieldwork in mundane settings, dealing with practical issues, and have little to do, if anything at all, with such abstract and transcendent ideas as Heidegger's 'nothing'. One could also argue perhaps that this attitude towards the unthought is largely a matter of personal disposition and character and does not necessarily enter into the ethnographer's professional life. Yet both objections would be unfounded. The 'heroisation' of the thinking subject is not only effected by elevated thinkers, nor is it a matter of idiosyncrasy and personal whim. On the contrary, it is an institutionalised feature of everyday academic practice – not just any feature, but one of the most fundamental. It is reproduced and propagated in what often goes by the name of 'critical thinking', itself the heart and soul of the teaching paradigm.[10] To underscore this point and to make the vital connection between a 'pure', elevated thinker and 'pragmatic' ethnographers and academics, between the eighteenth century and the present, I wish to return briefly to Kant and another of his essays entitled 'What is Orientation in Thinking?'

To think for oneself means to look within oneself (i.e. in one's own reason) for the supreme touchstone of the truth; and the maxim of thinking for oneself at all times is *enlightenment*. Now this requires less effort than is imagined by those who equate enlightenment with *knowledge*, for enlightenment consists rather in a negative principle in the use of one's cognitive powers, and those who are exceedingly rich in knowledge are often least enlightened in their use of it. (1970b [1786]: 249)

There are certain terms in this passage, such as 'enlightenment', which suggest that it may be from a text of another era. Otherwise, Kant's argument is a very precise and concise statement of what academics today mean by 'critical thinking'. To be a thinking person at all is to be critical, a person, that is, who refuses to take anything at face value. It really makes no difference what the source of a particular idea is, who authorises and sanctions it, how important it seems, or how old and established it may be. Thinking individuals would reflect on it and decide *by themselves* if it has any merit. This is what distinguishes such a person – the kind of person that Western academia aspires to produce – from those who are merely knowledgeable, those who know much but have no views of their own. This is also how the thinking person is valorised, 'heroised', indeed, virtually deified, how it learns to discover itself everywhere and at the bottom of everything, to be the basis and source of all Being – 'the supreme touchstone of the truth', as Kant put it – the very Subject of the world.

A few weeks after the event at Kykko monastery, the newspapers in Cyprus reported a similar event in another part of the island. A priest from a village near Nicosia, the capital of Cyprus, claimed that the icon of St George in the village church began to shed tears as well. Another miracle, another intervention of the divine in such a short timespan and in the same small and insignificant part of the world? Perhaps. Ethnographers, at any rate, could interpret this event along the same lines as the event at Kykko monastery, that is, as a symbolic phenomenon. They would treat it as a symbol – as something other than what it claims to be – because they know that miracles are not possible in our era, that the divine (if it exists) chooses to manifest itself through the laws of nature. Alternatively, ethnographers of the heterodox persuasion could refuse to interpret this and Other similar or dissimilar events and point out that any ethnological interpretation is bound to be 'fiction'. They would treat ethnological interpretations as a human invention because they know that 'immaculate conceptions' and representations are not possible in this world, that the divine (if it exists) is distant and indifferent to human affairs.

Ethnographers know such things because they are part of a culture in which people have mastered the courage to use their own understanding. And having done so, they now hold on to these disenchanting truths – they 'bear the fate of the times' – because in the heroic present of modernity the thinking subject must undertake the difficult task of re-Creating the world and itself. It must do so because its very autonomy and freedom is at stake. Such, at any rate, is the rhetoric. Ethnographers may know disenchanting things about native life; they may also know disenchanting things about their own lives. But the most fundamental and most enchanted of all things about themselves, they have not even begun to consider.

5   THE ETHNOLOGICAL WILL TO MEANING

THE IMPOSSIBLE

At the end of the second chapter of this book, I pointed out that it is not because they are Western that ethnographers divide the world. It is simply because they are. It is now time to unpack this statement and explain why human being – not being this or that particular subjectivity or socially and historically constituted identity, but being human as such – is in a certain fundamental sense, the root of the ethnological problem. With this we move away from epistemological considerations and into the realm of ontology itself. It is a shift away from questions about how ethnographers come to know Others to something prior to all empirical knowledge of this sort that acts as its condition of possibility, namely, the question of being a self or a consciousness aware of itself.

The discussion so far has shown that this move into the ontological domain is necessary, indeed, unavoidable. To begin with, it has shown that the epistemological problem raised by heterodox discourse is spurious. The truth about Others is not something that ethnographers may or may not be able to discover in the process of empirical investigation. This is a naive empiricist assumption that can no longer be defended. Rather, the truth about Others is something that ethnographers posit axiomatically, what makes empirical investigation into native lives possible to begin with. Ethnographers know a priori that Others are essentially and fundamentally the Same as them, and because they know and posit this as a categorical truth, the ethnological problem cannot be a problem of knowledge. As I have already suggested, what needs to be explained is how ethnographers, armed as they are with the truth about Others, end up dividing the world. It is this paradox that constitutes the essence of the ethnological problem and to explain this paradox it is necessary to look beyond epistemology.

The discussion so far has also taken a step towards completing its agonistic task, namely, to beat ethnological power at its own game, which is the game of knowledge. It has done so by breaking with the ethnological consensus, which is also a complicity, that links the problem of Otherness to the epistemological limits of ethnological discourse. It has ventured beyond the heterodox critique and has shown that despite epistemological limits, or perhaps because of them, all ethnographers without exception know the truth about Others: they are essentially and fundamentally the Same as 'us'.

If in their endeavour to demonstrate what they posit as the truth ethnographers reproduce its opposite, it must be because something else is involved, something prior to all epistemological considerations. To complete its agonistic task the present discourse must now explain what this 'something' is. In doing so, it will show what it is about themselves that the 'authorities' on ethnological knowledge don't know, that is, expose the nature of the ethnographer's own unconscious. The end of this explication – which would be an analysis as to why Sameness is impossible as well as why ethnographers must nonetheless persist in their efforts to win a battle that is always already lost – would also be the end of another round of the ethnological game. The next round will be played at the ethnographer's own risk.

I shall begin this excursion into the ethnological unconscious by making an apparently contradictory claim, namely, that the a priori representation of Sameness is impossible. But, the objection will no doubt immediately be raised, how can it be impossible if, as I claim here, it is the most fundamental ethnological representation? To be a representation at all, Sameness must exist, and if it exists, this is proof enough that it is possible. Yet to argue that Sameness is impossible is not to say that it is nothing; certainly, it is not to doubt the existence of the phenomenon, not to deny, that is, that ethnographers imagine, desire and posit something that they call Sameness. Indeed, I shall have more to say about the vantage point from which this something emerges as a reality in the next section. What is impossible, then, is not the phenomenon, but Sameness as such – not to say Sameness in-itself, which would be a contradictory statement. Sameness as such is impossible insofar as it cannot manifest itself in our world. This is to say that it cannot emerge in time or in consciousness because it occupies a place outside time and below consciousness. To be more precise, even though Sameness can be conceived and imagined (since we all know what it means) this can be done only at an instant – a strange instant, no doubt, because it both allows Sameness to come forward into the world and utterly destroys it at the very same moment.

I wish first to sketch the structural movements of the impossibility of demonstrating Sameness and then try to explain the ontological condition of possibility of this impossibility. But before I turn to this task, it may be useful to discuss by way of comparison the impossibility of something that is of the same order and nature as Sameness, namely, gift-giving.

'Whenever there is time', Derrida (1992: 9) points out, 'the gift is impossible'. It is impossible precisely because time (or self-consciousness) is what is required for those involved in the cycle of gift exchange to become aware of it as gift. When they do become aware of it as such, which is always, a gift is no longer 'gift'. It becomes something entirely different. A gift should be given with no ulterior motives in mind, without any expectation of return, and should not be reciprocated in any way whatsoever. Such are the constitutive rules of this particular game, what make a gift 'gift' and distinguish it from a loan, an investment or a market exchange. What this means, Derrida points out, is that gift-givers must not recognise what they give as gift; they must be completely oblivious to their giving as gift-giving. For even the pleasure of giving is enough to destroy the gift, since the gift-giver now receives something in return. Nor should gift-receivers recognise what they receive as gift; they too must be completely oblivious to their receiving as accepting a gift. If they so recognise it, as always happens, the gift is utterly destroyed; it becomes a *debt* to be repaid in the form of a counter-gift. Because there is time, then – or consciousness that makes time[1] – the gift as such is, paradoxically enough, impossible.

Much the same argument can be made about Sameness itself. For Sameness to manifest itself in the world, ethnographers must constitute difference as that which does not know itself. As I have argued in the last chapter, they must posit a native sociocultural unconscious. Ethnographers must do so for a simple reason: if difference knew the truth about itself or, at any rate, what ethnographers claim to be the truth, it would cease being different and become the Same – in which case the ethnological enterprise would have no reason to exist. If the Zande were persuaded to adopt the truth that Evans-Pritchard posited about witchcraft, they would lose faith in it – the same way in which Evans-Pritchard lost faith in Catholicism. They would no longer explain the collapse of their granaries like Zande, but very much like the ethnographer, which means that Evans-Pritchard would have no reason to make an ethnological issue out of their explanation.

If difference does not know itself, then, Sameness begins to manifest itself. Rather than being irrational or pre-logical, the Zande now appear sensible and rational like 'us'. No doubt, they are still different – they still explain misfortune in terms of witchcraft while the ethnographer explains it as an accident – but this is not a fundamental difference. The Azande are different only in form, since the content of their belief in witchcraft is now shown to be the Same as the ethnographer's. And yet, as soon as Sameness begins to emerge in this way, it is at the very same instant crushed by its own weight. There is no time whatsoever for Sameness to unfold itself before it turns into difference. In no time, it transforms itself into the difference that now exists between the ethnographer who knows the truth of Otherness – that it is, in fact, the Same – and the Zande who do not and, as the ethnological explanation suggests, cannot know this truth. For an instant, the Zande become the Same as 'us' because they are shown to be sensible and reasonable, but at the very same instant they also become different because unlike 'us', they do not know how sensible and reasonable they are. They think of witchcraft as a bodily substance with malevolent intent when 'in fact' it is only a symbol, a reasonable way of explaining misfortune.

Heterodox discourse encounters the same ontological wall and crashes in a similar way. The structural movements that lead to the impossible in this case can be sketched out as follows. For Sameness to manifest itself in the world, heterodox ethnographers must constitute anthropology as a system of thought and practice that knows the truth about itself, namely, that ethnological representations are very much a part of this world and, as such, are mediated by 'rhetoric' and 'power'. They must constitute anthropology as a self-reflective, fully conscious system because, as long as the discipline does not come to terms with the limits of representation, it would continue producing and reproducing Otherness and difference. If anthropology knows the truth about itself – that Otherness is 'fiction' or 'poetry' – Sameness begins to manifest itself. But before it has any time whatsoever to emerge into the world, it expires. It is as though it becomes dazzled by its own brilliant light and retreats into the shadows again. Sameness is instantly destroyed because anthropology has now become essentially and fundamentally different from all those cultural systems, such as Zande witchcraft, that it studies. It has become different because it is now fully aware of its truth, while Zande witchcraft remains oblivious to its own. The discipline has now entered into an asymmetrical relationship with Other cultural systems and is confronting them as consciousness is facing the unconscious, courage is facing cowardice and autonomy is facing dependence and subordination.

To generalise the argument, Sameness is impossible precisely because it is 'we' who constitute it as a reality of this world – 'we' being whoever imagines, desires, posits and, as in the case of ethnographers, strives to demonstrate Sameness. This 'we' is not as simple as it might seem. It is an impossible double persona: we as part of the reality we describe, and we as those who posit this reality; we within a world of Sameness, and we outside this world demarcating its boundaries and putting them in place. This 'we' is impossible precisely because, by positing Sameness, ethnographers instantly and inevitably bracket themselves off from what they posit. They become the creators of a world of Sameness, which means that they establish a relation of difference with the world – even if the relation they posit for everyone else is one of Sameness – the sort of asymmetrical relationship that connects the creator with its creations. Ethnographers, then, are caught in the doubt bind of trying to be both creators of a world of Sameness and at the same time creatures in the world they have created or, as Foucault (1970) would say, both 'subjects and objects' – which is impossible.

It is true of course that ethnographers include their own culture – which is both the anthropological culture and the culture of the anthropologist – in this domain of Sameness. But this inclusion is nothing more than an illusion. If it is possible at all to make this claim, it is only because ethnographers efface from their memory the inaugural act of positing a world in which all cultures embody the Same value, only because they conveniently forget that it is *they* who construct the world in this way. The inaugural act of positing Sameness places all cultures at the same level of value, *except* the anthropological culture and the culture of the anthropologist. The latter becomes a culture of superior value, if not for any other reason, because it is the culture that sets the system of cultural value in place.

There is, then, a threshold of consciousness that Sameness is forever forbidden from crossing – a threshold that make Sameness an utter impossibility. Ethnographers may conveniently forget that it is they who construct a world of Sameness, but this forgetting *already* means that the critical threshold of consciousness has been crossed, that Sameness has *already* been destroyed. Forgetting is always already too late. What is required is complete obliviousness. Indeed, to make another paradoxical statement, the only proof that Sameness may be present in the world is our utter and permanent ignorance of its existence. To say this, of course, is to argue that Sameness can never manifest itself to us, that it can manifest itself only to an outside observer who is not, and will *never* be one of us, that is, to someone who will always be different – God, let us say, or a being from another world. To such an outside observer, we may all be the Same. Such a being can observe and stand witness to our Sameness, and by doing so to the difference that separates it from us. By positing Sameness, ethnographers assume the position and point of view of such a cosmic observer. They observe and stand witness to the Sameness of everyone below – everyone, that is, except themselves.

All this goes to show that the limit of Sameness is that it can manifest itself only on the condition that it creates difference – on the condition, that is, that it destroys itself in emergence – which is another way of saying that it cannot manifest itself. What remains to be explained is the nature of this limit on Sameness and other impossibilities such as gift exchange. What is it that sets this sort of limit on the world? And is there any way to overcome it? To answer these questions, I shall turn to Sartre's (1958 [1943]) seminal work, *Being and Nothingness*, and particularly to his discussion on the nature of consciousness and the self. What Sartre has to say about these issues has been in many respects anticipated by several other thinkers, including Durkheim (1915) in his outline of a sociology of knowledge and Lévy-Bruhl (1925) in his discussion on 'how natives think'. Even closer to contemporary anthropology, Geertz's (1973a) theory of culture is based on the same sort of fundamental distinctions as those found in Sartre. If I turn to Sartre's work, it is only because it makes explicit the kind of argument that I wish to pursue here.

For Sartre, as well as for Husserl and Heidegger before him, consciousness is always consciousness of something. This means that consciousness can be aware of itself, that is, become self-conscious only by means of something that is not consciousness. Consciousness reflecting on itself immediately and directly, without the presence of a mediating term, is an impossibility. There must be something outside itself on which to reflect, even if that something is nothing other than the notion of consciousness posited as an object of reflection. In other words, there must be some way in which consciousness can distinguish itself from what it is, a certain space to separate it from itself and to prevent it from collapsing onto itself. As Sartre puts it, 'the being of consciousness qua consciousness is to exist *at a distance from itself* as a presence to itself' (1958: 78). The distance that separates consciousness from itself, Sartre calls 'nothingness', since, as he points out, there is really nothing between consciousness and itself. This 'nothingness', however, is not a figment of the imagination but an ontological necessity. Without it, consciousness would coincide with itself to such an extent that it would annihilate itself in the process. It would merge with itself into complete and indistinguishable unity and hence cease being what it was before the fusion. It would, in short, achieve absolute identity with itself and therefore lose its own identity, which is none other than awareness of being a consciousness – self-consciousness.

Consciousness, then, exists and can exist only as negation, that is, by creating difference. To be self-conscious is to be aware that one is NOT – not what is present to one's consciousness, not this or that thing in the world, not the 'same'. Hence, for Sartre, negation is determination – denial that one is this or that thing in the world is at the same time affirmation that (of what) one is. Without negation of the world one would not be aware of one's own existence, which is to say, one would not be (a self-conscious being). This means that difference, or 'ontological separation' as Sartre calls the outcome of being self-conscious, is an inescapable fact of the world.

Sartre's argument about the nature of self-consciousness may not be agreeable to those who strive to demonstrate the 'ontological unity' of the world, but ethnographers are hardly strangers to it. Most have come across it by means of another route and in a different guise, namely, Evans-Pritchard's confrontation with Lévy-Bruhl and the latter's notorious 'law of participation'. Indeed, what Lévy-Bruhl imagines about 'primitive mentality' is more or less the reverse of what Sartre posits as the condition of possibility of self-consciousness. If for Sartre self-consciousness is consciousness of not being this or that thing in the world, for Lévy-Bruhl 'primitive mentality' is characterised precisely by a readiness to be this or that – the totem of the tribe, for instance, or one's shadow. Hence his insistence that natives are indifferent to the law of contradiction and the argument that their mentality is 'pre-logical'. This is not to say 'pre-modern', since, for Lévy-Bruhl, the 'law of participation' constitutes a native universe different even from the world of pre-modern Europe.

By way of contrast, here is how Foucault explains the delicate balance between two world-structuring principles in sixteenth-century Europe – 'sympathy' and 'antipathy'. The former, Foucault points out:

has the dangerous power of *assimilating*, of rendering things identical to one another, of mingling them, of causing their individuality to disappear – and thus of rendering them foreign to what they were before. Sympathy transforms. It alters, but in the direction of identity, so that if its power were not counterbalanced, it would reduce the world to a point, to a homogeneous mass, to the featureless form of the Same. (1970: 23–4)

If it were left to its own devices, then, 'sympathy' would destroy the world. Luckily, it is not allowed such freedom, since it is always counterbalanced by the opposite principle, 'antipathy'. The latter, Foucault (1970: 24) points out, 'maintains the isolation of things and prevents their assimilation; it encloses every species within its impenetrable difference and its propensity to continue being what it is'. By contrast, Lévy-Bruhl is not prepared to grant 'primitive mentality' such distinguishing capabilities. The 'law of participation' knows nothing of 'antipathy', and there is nothing else in Lévy-Bruhl's system to keep its 'sympathetic' impulsiveness in check. Under such conditions, one does not experience oneself as being part of the world, but rather as being *one* with the world. Indeed, for Lévy-Bruhl primitive 'participation in [the world] is so effectively *lived* that [the world] is not yet properly imagined' (1925: 362). To say this, of course, is to suggest that 'natives' are not 'properly' conscious of themselves, that is, self-conscious. In effect, it is to de-humanise them.[2]

Ethnographers are not strangers to the idea that self-consciousness exists only insofar as it is mediated because of contemporary theories of the origins and nature of culture as well. As I have already suggested, Geertz (1973a) argues that there are two sources of information – 'intrinsic' and 'extrinsic'. The former, which is common to both human beings and animals, refers to instincts, that is, to information that is inaccessible to self-consciousness. Extrinsic information, on the other hand, is uniquely human and refers to information purposely created, that is, to ideas. As Geertz points out, extrinsic information is deposited in symbols, and a system of symbols makes up a culture. Now symbols are precisely the means by which consciousness becomes aware of itself – a self-consciousness. They are what mediates between consciousness and itself, what allows consciousness to put a certain distance between it and itself so that it can look back on itself and become aware that it exists. It is by investing itself into something that is NOT consciousness – a symbol – that human consciousness becomes what it is. Human knowledge, then, self-knowledge as well as knowledge of anything else, is by its very nature mediated and symbolic.

In the section of *Being and Nothingness* entitled 'The Existence of Others', Sartre points out that the negative structure he identified as the constitutive element of consciousness applies as much to the construction of the self. If to be conscious is to be aware that one is not this or that object in the world, to be a self and to have an identity is to be aware that one is not this or that person in the world – not the other.[3] Here is how Sartre (1958: 283) puts the matter:

> The For-itself [the self] which I am simply has to be what it is in the form of a refusal of the other; that is, as itself. Thus by utilizing the formulae applied to the knowledge of the Not-me in general, we can say that the For-itself as itself includes the being of the other in its being in so far as its being is in question as not being the other.

Sartre's neologisms and play with words aside, there is really nothing unfamiliar about this argument. In effect, it suggests that identity is relational and exclusive, an argument with which ethnographers are well acquainted. As is often pointed out, for example, the West as an identity exists and has significance only in relation to the Other, that is, only insofar as it excludes the Other. This is not to say that West and Other as cultural definitions of selfhood are completely dissimilar; it is to say rather that they can never be identical. If they became the Same, it would not be possible to tell them apart. They would fuse into an undifferentiated whole and simply cease being distinct identities. To put it in another way, if the Western self did not exist in the form of not being the Other, it would not be able to say what sort of self it is. At the limit, it would not be able to say that it is a self at all.

In the same section, Sartre provides a certain qualification about the relation between self and other that I wish to explore here briefly, since it will constitute the basis of subsequent discussion. Not being the other, Sartre points out, is not exactly the same thing as not being this or that thing in the world. The other is itself a self and a subjectivity. This means that, in the case of the other, the negative structure of not being this or that thing in the world, which determines the self and constitutes difference, is reciprocated. To be itself, a thing does not need to negate anything; it is enough that it is negated by human consciousness. The other, however, being a subjectivity and not a thing, must negate some other subjectivity, since, by definition, this is the only way in which it can be a self. Thus, if I am not the other in order to be myself, the other must not be me in order to be itself.

What is significant about this doubly negative structure for the purposes of the present discussion is that it raises the possibility of a certain equality between West and Other as cultural identities. If it is true that to be Western one must not be the Other, it is equally true that to be itself the Other must exclude the West. It may be recalled that one of Said's main arguments in *Orientalism* is that the West as an identity gains in strength by constructing the Orient as an underground image of itself. On the basis of the doubly negative structure identified by Sartre, however, one could plausibly argue that the Orient gains as much in strength by constructing the West as an underground image of *itself*. Does this not mean that a certain balance in terms of exclusion and a certain equality in terms of identity strength are achieved? I shall return to this important question below. But first, in the light of what has been said so far, it may be useful at this point to return to the question of the ethnological problem and reiterate the priority of ontological separation over the divisions that ethnographers effect in the course of their empirical investigations.

The ontological separation between the self and the world, that is, the establishment of ontological difference, precedes and makes possible any form of empirical knowledge about the world. One must first be a self in order to become a subject of knowledge. To know the nature of the object that one is dealing with – its properties, for example – and to understand how this object is related to other objects, it is necessary to become aware that the object is an entity distinct from oneself.[4] In a similar vein, to know who others are and how they relate among themselves as well as to oneself, it is necessary to know first that they are other. Hence, empirical knowledge of others presupposes an ontological division between them and oneself. This means that any epistemological critique of anthropology as a corrective to the divisions that the discipline effects, such as the heterodox critique, must fail. To be sure, one cannot be a Western self without excluding the Other, but this does not mean that by denying this identity one arrives at a unified world. Ethnographers detach themselves from their social and historical circumstances – from their Westernness – if not completely (for this is not possible) certainly to a far greater extent than other Westerners. They posit Sameness, perhaps the most universal statement that one can make about the self and Others. Yet, as I have already shown, even Sameness does not eradicate the division between the two – it reproduces it. The point, then, is not how wide and inclusive an identity one is able to construct for oneself. It is rather that one is a self and has identity. In this sense, ethnographers divide the world not because they are Western, but because they are. The division they effect is first and foremost ontological and only secondarily and derivatively the outcome of epistemological constraints. Without ontological separation there can be no other division.

Having arrived at this conclusion, it is necessary to point out that there is a sense, and an important one at that, in which being Western is highly significant and comes to bear heavily on the divisions of the world or, at any rate, more heavily than being Other. To say this is not to deny what has just been asserted – the priority of ontological division and difference. It is to say rather that, in practice, ontological separations that go into the construction of cultural selves and geopolitical identities do not carry the same weight. As I have already suggested, in Sartre's scheme, to be myself, I must refuse the other, and to be itself the other must refuse me. In this doubly negative structure there appears to be reciprocity in refusal and a certain parity in being a self and having an identity. Indeed, for Sartre this structure demonstrates that the other cannot or, at any rate, should not be treated as an object. Sartre spends an inordinate amount of time on this otherwise straightforward point and in this one senses the anxiety of the humanist trying to make an airtight case for the other. Yet, even though on logical grounds Sartre's argument is unassailable, in practice it does not work. If one employs the term other in its ethnological sense, that is, to refer specifically to the non-West, it soon becomes apparent that Sartre's theoretical scheme breaks down.

To begin with, there are certain Others who do not refuse the West. Indeed, if anything, they aspire to become part of it. What I have in mind here is the urban middle classes in Cyprus, but apparently Western-oriented elites exist in every part of the world. To say that certain Others do not refuse the West is not to say, of course, that they are left with no sense of self and no cultural identity. The Cypriot urban middle classes, for example, become what they are (or strive to become what they aspire to be) by refusing the Other within Cyprus – the case of the event at Kykko monastery discussed in the last chapter, where all those who 'flocked' to the monastery accepted the event as a miracle, but, in more general terms, villagers and the urban working classes.[5] There is, then, a tendency among elites to endorse rather than deny the West and hence a breakdown of reciprocity in refusal, since these Others must be, and are in fact refused by the West.[6] As for those Others who do refuse the West, whether explicitly or symbolically, it is not at all certain that they thereby achieve parity in cultural being. No doubt, West and Other are both identities, but do they carry the same weight? Is refusal of the West by the Other as compelling an event as refusal of the Other by the West? In short, does denial of being the West constitute the Other as an identity of equal strength and standing?

The best way to answer these questions is to examine ethnological discourses that deal specifically with the Other's refusal of the West – which are often celebrated by ethnographers as 'resistance' to Western encroachment. I shall explore briefly two well-known books, Michael Taussig's *The Devil and Commodity Fetishism in South America* (1980) and Aihwa Ong's *Spirits of Resistance and Capitalist Discipline* (1987), but there are many other similar works in the ethnological literature.[7] Both books show how local populations – in the first case South American peasants and miners, in the second Malay peasant women – employ certain core elements of their respective cultures to make sense of and resist the imposition of capitalism and its culture. How far, then, do such practices of negation act as determinations of autonomous subjectivity? How do the local identities to which these people still cling fare with the identities they refuse?

In Taussig's book the organising theme is the devil. In sugar plantations, for example, workers enter into a secret contract with the devil in the hope that with its help, they will be able to work faster and increase their wages. As people say, however, any extra money earned in this way does not make one's life better. It is spent on luxuries, and those who make such pacts with the devil often die premature and painful deaths. For Taussig (1980: 7) what appears to be mere superstition is in fact the way in which local people publicise 'their own criticisms of the forces that are affecting their society – forces which emanate from us'. These forces are none other than the capitalist relations of production. Local people criticise the alienation that they now experience, having been uprooted from their land and their communities, the fabric of social relations based on reciprocity and gift exchange having been destroyed and replaced by relations based on personal interest and greed. People may now have more money but, as the devil story vividly illustrates, they feel that they lead poorer lives. The devil, then, is a critique of commodity fetishism, 'an image *illuminating* a culture's *self-consciousness* of the threat posed to its integrity' (1980: 96; my emphases). As a critique and refusal of the West, it is also, inextricably, an attempt to define the self, or rather to redefine it on the basis of what it has once been. As Taussig (1980: 96) himself argues, the devil contract is a '"text" in which is inscribed a culture's attempt to redeem its history by reconstituting the significance of the past in terms of the tensions of the present'.

In a similar vein, Ong tells the story of young Malay women of peasant background who become factory workers. On the whole, these young women are model workers: self-composed, obedient and hard-working. Nonetheless, many are often seized by spirits on the shopfloor and lose their self-control, become violent and scream abuses at their superiors. The rural Malay universe in which these women originate, Ong (1987: 203) explains, 'is still inhabited by spirits which move easily between human and nonhuman domains'. These young women are using a culturally familiar idiom to articulate their experience in a new, unfamiliar and oppressive work environment. This, according to Ong, is not to say that in the familiar rural setting women were not subjected to relations of power and domination. Indeed, patriarchal authority and male domination are widespread. In their daily activities, however, they were largely free of control. As Ong (1987: 168) points out, in 'village social contexts ... women were seldom monitored by someone in their work but enjoyed self-determination'. The spirits that possess the young Malay factory workers, then, express the spirit of resistance to the de-humanising capitalist discipline on the shopfloor – 'the rigidity of work routine, continual male supervision, and devaluation of their labor in the factory'. It is 'a protest against the loss of autonomy/humanity in work' (Ong 1987: 7–8).

We have, then, two well-documented cases in which the Other is refusing the West in order to be itself – two cases of refusal that, interestingly enough, are celebrated by those whose way of life is refused. What the Other is refusing in both cases is quite clear: it is the 'de-humanising' nature of Western capitalism. What it tries to maintain by means of this refusal is also quite clear: it is a cultural universe in which social relations are not reduced to relations between things, where people do not take second place to money. In short, the Other tries to maintain its 'humanity'. To what extent, then, do these refusals constitute the Other as an autonomous subjectivity? How does the identity that these refusals try to maintain fare in relation to the identity refused?

Let us first note that what the Other is refusing is exactly what those celebrating the refusal – left-wing, liberal ethnographers – have themselves already refused. Indeed, what appears to the ethnographer to be rejected in the devil contract and episodes of spirit possession – commodity fetishism and capitalist discipline – are Western cultural constructs that have been developed and used specifically for purposes of self-criticism. Let us also note that that for the sake of which (according to the ethnographer, at any rate) Others are struggling, namely, autonomy and human dignity, are themselves Western cultural constructs – the product of the Enlightenment – and constitute the core of modern Western ideology. It is not at all clear, then, that Others constitute themselves as autonomous subjectivities automatic-ally, as Sartre's formula would predict, that is, by merely asserting that they are not the West. Indeed, it begins to look as though, insofar as they become subjectivities – they acquire a voice and an identity – this is not because of their refusal of the West as such. Rather, it appears that it is because their refusal (if refusal it is) is endorsed and consecrated by outside authorities –

by the liberal, left-wing ethnographer in the first instance and, second, by the West's own institutionalised refusal of its de-humanising aspects. This question can only be settled by examining situations in which the Other's refusal is itself refused and rejected by outside authorities. Luckily, both ethnographies under consideration provide clear illustrations of such cases.

South American peasants and miners and young Malay women are resisting capitalism and its discipline on the basis of their own culture. They are refusing the West in order to be themselves and are doing so by actually being themselves, that is, by articulating their rejection through metaphysical constructs such as the devil and other malevolent spirits. But although the aim of the Other's refusal of the West is celebrated by the ethnographer, the mode in which this refusal is expressed is rejected. It is rejected even though it is as much part of the Other's culture as the identity that the Other's refusal supposedly strives to maintain. This rejection by the ethnographer should not be surprising. The mode in which the Other's refusal is expressed has long been discredited in the West, not only by materialist Marxists, but also by empiricists and rationalists of every colour and persuasion. It has been discredited, not only because it employs metaphysical constructs, but also because it is symbolic. Being a symbolic mode of thought, it distorts the realities of capitalism which now appear as the devil or other malevolent spirits. In short, this mode of dealing with reality misinterprets the world. Here is how Taussig himself puts the matter in the concluding pages of his book:

In a myriad of *improbable* ways, magic and rite can strengthen the critical conscious-ness that a devastatingly hostile reality forces on the people laboring in the plantations and mines. Without the legacy of culture and without its rhetorical figures, images, fables, metaphors, and other imaginative creations, this consciousness cannot function. Yet it can be made *aware* of its creative powers instead of ascribing that power to its products. Social progress and critical thought are bound to this dialectical task of *defetishization*. (1980: 232; my emphases)

What Taussig gives with one hand he takes away with the other. The Other's consciousness cannot function without culture, even when the culture in question is based on 'fables' and myths. But this does not mean that it functions well. Indeed, to the extent that such fables and myths contribute to the raising of the Other's consciousness, they do so only in 'improbable' ways. What, then, can the Other do to secure the development of its consciousness so that it becomes 'critical'? It must, Taussig makes clear, cast 'fetishes' aside and recognise that the powers of its 'imaginative creations' are in fact its own powers. It must go beyond the symbol, as Durkheim would say, to the reality that is hiding underneath. If it does so, it will see, as clearly as Taussig does, that there are no devils in the world except capitalism and its de-humanising relations.

Ong makes an even stronger case for the need to develop a critical (as opposed to symbolic) consciousness. Speaking about the position of women in Malay society, Ong (1987: 193) points out that 'it did not occur to any factory woman to question the overall male-dominated systems in the household, factory, religion, and wider society'. This does not mean, of course, that they have no voice at all to speak about their domination. In the factories, they often speak with the voice of spirits, and what they say is heard loudly enough. But this is not their own voice, nor is the language they use what should be used in reflecting about, and articulating problems with one's conditions of existence. It is a symbolic language that covers over what must be thought of analytically and communicated clearly. As Ong (1987: 210) argues, these women's reaction to capitalist discipline and male domination is a 'ritualised rebellion' and as such 'did not directly confront the real causes of their distress'. In fact, not only did it fail to do so, but also 'by operating as a safety valve, tended to reinforce existing unequal relations which are further legitimised by scientific notions of female maladjustment'. The spirits, then, are not helping out, after all. On the contrary, they act as a screen that hides from these women the real cause of their problem; and they make the situation even worse by confirming the sexist ideology that women are emotional creatures who require male supervision and control. In short, these women's protest is a symbolic, ritualised rebellion that cannot transform the real world.

It is certainly interesting that both ethnographers call for an urgent raising of the Other's consciousness. As I have argued in the last chapter, ethnographers usually posit a native sociocultural unconscious and leave the matter at that. But these two cases are instances of a more activist ethnography, an attempt to save Others not only symbolically but also practically. Be that as it may, it is now clear that in both cases the means by which the Other refuses the West – and hence the means by which it tries to be itself – are not sanctioned by the ethnographer. It should also be clear that because these symbolic means are not sanctioned, the Other is NOT, even though this is how it refuses the West and hence, as far as it is concerned, IT IS. The Other, according to the ethnographer, is *not* 'aware of its creative powers', *not* 'confronting directly the causes of its distress', *not* fully conscious of its real conditions of existence and certainly *not* in possession of a 'critical' consciousness. The Other is not, but is becoming – perhaps. The Other is still not a self and not itself, even though its assertion that it is not the West should be enough, according to Sartre's formula at any rate, to constitute it as an autonomous subjectivity. But this selfhood that the Other no doubt is, is not sanctioned by the authorities that sanction and legitimise, and because it is not sanctioned, the Other is still NOT. It is still not a cultural identity of the same standing, gravity and import as the identity that it refuses to become.

To conclude this section on the impossibility of Sameness and the inevitability of division, let me first reiterate what has already been said – that the condition of possibility of any division in the world and hence of any sort of identity is the original ontological separation between self and the world. Now if this ontological separation is the inevitable outcome of being a human being, being European or American is of no consequence. All

human beings are by definition involved in the process of dividing the world
along one line or another, all have equal access to the means by which the
world is divided. This pluralism, however, breaks down in practice, since it
is one thing to divide the world and quite another to constitute one's divisions
as appropriate and legitimate. To be effective, divisions require recognition
not only by those who effect them but also, and more importantly, by those
who bear the consequences. In this respect, being European or American is
highly significant.

The West has established itself as the primary source of legitimate signifi-
cation and monopolises the means of symbolic production. To say this is not
to argue that whatever Europeans or Americans say about the world is
bound to be recognised by Others as a legitimate statement. Rather, it is to
argue first, that being Western authorises one to speak or, at any rate,
authorises one to a far greater extent than being Other; and second, that the
language of the West – whether this goes by the name of rationality or
science – is by means of the recognition accorded to it already predisposed
to produce legitimate statements. Indeed, it is predisposed to do so even
when, as in the case of 'postmodern' discourse, the statements produced are
highly critical of both rationality and science. It is true, then, to say that
ethnographers divide the world not because they are Western, but simply
because they are. But it is equally true to say that by being Western, their
divisions come to bear far more heavily on the world that the divisions
effected by any Other.

SAMENESS AND THE BEYOND

Sameness is impossible. Even though it is not nothing, it can never manifest
itself in our world. Indeed, what manifests itself, what we observe and witness
in everyday life is not Sameness but its contrary – Otherness and difference.
Yet ethnographers imagine, desire and posit Sameness as a reality of this
world; and they strive to uphold it by devising ingenious formulas and
strategies for redeeming Others. Why is it, then, that ethnographers persist
in desiring what, by definition, they must not, and cannot be? Why do they
persist in positing this non-entity as a reality in the world, when the only
reality that they perceive and experience contradicts it so blatantly? Why do
they persist in trying to demonstrate Sameness when past experience shows
that all such attempts have done little more than to reproduce its contrary?

To address this question, it is necessary to examine the conditions of
possibility of this impossibility that we call Sameness. We must begin
searching for that position which one must occupy in order to name the
impossible, for that vantage point from which we all appear to be the Same
– all the Same in an instant, that is, and then at that very moment all the
Same except those to whom, at that instant, Sameness is visible. In this
strange search for the impossible, I will use as a rough guide three

ethnographic illustrations or vignettes from the Greek-speaking world. The first of these vignettes comes from Athens, the second from an unidentified place at sea somewhere between Athens' port, Pireas, and the island of Crete, and the third from further east in the Mediterranean, the island of Cyprus.

I shall begin with the lyrics of a song by the popular Greek singer, gypsy (but long-time resident of Athens), devout Christian and fierce critic of modern Greek life, Costas Hadjis. The song, which was particularly popular in the 1970s, is entitled 'The Aeroplane'.

> When you fly, from high up the world looks like a painting
> and you took it seriously!
> Towers look like matchboxes and people like ants
> The largest palace looks like a child's football.
> My dearest, don't cry. If you like, come high up as well
> to see the Earth from the Moon; it too is a moon.

In this song, Hadjis is asking a friend who seems to have been hurt by life's blows to fly with him in an aeroplane. From a vantage point high up in the air, the world looks very different; it looks so different, in fact, that it can no longer be taken 'seriously'. It is just like the Moon – a moon rather than a planet, a place of no particular importance rather than, as we often like to think, the centre of the universe. In this rather unimportant place, the mighty and the wealthy, symbolised in the song by towers and palaces, those who have the power to hurt and make people 'cry', appear small and insignificant. The perspective from high up in the air reduces their status to its 'true' dimensions so that they now emerge as no more threatening and dangerous than children's toys. Indeed, from such a perspective, we all appear small, insignificant and indistinguishable from one another – just like so many 'ants' – absorbed in our daily affairs, oblivious to the wider realities of the world.

There are, then, two possible visions of the world, according to the song, two images that are made possible by two rather different positions. The first position is on the ground, and from here life appears as we know it – unjust, ugly and capable of causing pain and suffering. This vision of the world should not be taken seriously, according to Hadjis; it is appearance, not reality. The second position is high above the ground, in the air, outside of the world. This position affords a clearer picture of life and reveals the true nature of things. It shows that all distinctions, divisions and differences are spurious and that in the wider scheme of things – in reality – we are all the Same small and insignificant creatures. It would seem, then, that a vantage point from outside the world has a levelling effect; it operates as an equaliser of all human disparities.

The second vignette is from Nicos Kazantzakis's well-known novel, *The Life and Times of Alexis Zorba*.[8] Kazantzakis, a writer, intellectual and would-be businessman, meets Zorba at a coffee house in Pireas, Athens' port. He is waiting to take the boat to Crete where he has bought an old coal mine, is taken in by Zorba's manner and spirited ways and decides to take him along to assist with the mine project. In the following extract, they are already on the boat sailing for Crete and Zorba, a mountain man, is struggling with sea-sickness. Kazantzakis on the hand, an islander and native of Crete, is standing on deck enjoying the sea, the breeze and the sunshine after a brief storm. He is trying to get away as much as possible from his fellow passengers, 'the sly Greeks with rapacious eyes, the petty minds, and their quarrels about trivial political matters ... the virtuous venomous shrews, the cruel, dull provinciality'. Kazantzakis, who has long elevated himself above such meanness and pettiness, imagines seizing the boat and plunging it into the sea to clean it from all living beings that 'polluted' it with their presence – both people and animals. But at the same time, he cannot help feeling a certain compassion for what he sees, 'a cold, Buddhist compassion, the outcome of complicated metaphysical reflection; compassion, not only for people, but for the entire world that struggles, cries, weeps, hopes, and does not realise that everything is a spectacular illusion – Nothingness' (1973: 30–1).

In this brief passage, we can once again discern two conflicting ways of looking at the world. The first refers to the vision of Kazantzakis's fellow passengers, who, as the author suggests, typify what it means to be Greek, and the second to his own worldview. Kazantzakis's prose is rich in metaphor and imagery, and, to get to the vision of the world that he ascribes to modern Greeks, it is necessary to look at some of his expressions in greater detail. His Greeks, then, are 'sly', out to deceive and take advantage of others, and have 'petty minds' – minds that, when it comes to personal gain, will calculate and take stock of everything, even the smallest of things. This image is made even stronger by the expression 'rapacious eyes', eyes that scrutinise everything, not out of curiosity, but with the intent to seize whatever can be seized. Indeed, the Greek term that I here translate as rapacious – *arpakhtika* – literally means snatching. More significantly still, it is often used in the expression *arpakhtika poulia*, meaning 'birds of prey'. I should also briefly discuss the expression 'virtuous venomous shrews', which Kazantzakis is using to refer to the women on the boat. To begin with, the term 'virtuous' (*timies*) is meant to refer to female sexual modesty.[9] Such women are very much concerned with upholding the community's moral standards, and do so with such zeal, it would seem, that they end up becoming 'venomous shrews'. They acquire a tongue that spits poison, meaning that they are highly critical of other women who may not uphold the same standards, and implying that they may also go so far as to fabricate stories and spread rumors about other women's virtue with the intent of damaging the latter's reputation. In short, the expression points to the same readiness encountered in Greek men's alleged attitude to seize and appropriate for themselves what belongs to others.

We have, then, the picture of a world in which people are totally immersed in the here and now, have invested heavily in the stakes of everyday life, whether material or symbolic, and are now striving to take advantage of others by whatever means available – a picture, in other words, in which people are unable to see beyond their petty personal interests or rise above their parochial world. Kazantzakis's own vision of life on the other hand is totally different. To begin with, it is a vision from a vantage point outside the world, not just the Greek world of his fellow passengers, but the world at large. From this vantage point Kazantzakis sees 'the entire world' struggling, crying and hoping, and feels deep compassion for it. It is the compassion of a Buddha who has seen the light and now feels pity for those who are blind to it. He feels pity because the struggle for existence and everything it entails – calculation, competition, division, domination over things and people – are absurd and meaningless; because all the time and energy invested in this struggle, all the wealth and power accumulated, all the pain and suffering caused to others are for nothing. They are for nothing, since in the wider scheme of things, life itself is 'Nothing'.

The last vignette comes from the island of Cyprus and has to do with death, particularly the death of the wealthy, the powerful and the distinguished. When it becomes known that such people have died, ordinary folk often remark: 'Rich and poor, we'll all be eaten by the same soil'; or that 'No one takes anything with him; we are all left with two metres of earth.'[10] There is a certain philosophical posture in such comments which is prompted by death and reveals the need of ordinary people to pause and reflect on the meaning of life; or rather, to be more precise, it reveals the need to remember what is already known but somehow forgotten in the business of everyday life. But beyond this, comments of this sort serve a specific social and political purpose. They are meant to highlight the futility and absurdity of the struggle to accumulate wealth and power, since these things are temporary and none survives death; and to remind those who may have forgotten that all people – rich and poor, important and unimportant – are essentially and fundamentally equal. In the face of death, such divisions are completely effaced and what remains is the Same for all, two metres of earth – the grave.

It is now possible to return to the question I have raised concerning the conditions of possibility of what ethnographers think of as Sameness and try to address it. We are looking for a position from which one could catch sight of Sameness – for a mere instant, no doubt, which is not an instant of ordinary time – for the vantage point from which we all appear to be the Same. All three vignettes indicate that this strange place is located somewhere *beyond* the world, that we are dealing in effect with a *metaphysical* position. In the first vignette, Hadjis locates his own position with the help of a convenient spatial metaphor. He sees that palaces and towers are mere children's toys and people like ants from the aeroplane; he sees that the Earth is only a moon, rather than the centre of the universe, from the Moon itself.

The objection could be raised, perhaps, that the aeroplane and the Moon express real distance and hence are not metaphors at all. People fly every day, and although not many have visited the Moon, most have access to such a view of the Earth from the photographs taken by those who have been there. Surely, there is nothing metaphysical about that. It is true, of course, that people fly every day and that the distance between the Earth and the Moon has been precisely calculated. The point, however, is that from no altitude above the Earth can palaces and towers ever be transformed into children's toys, that is, power into something as innocuous as that. Nor can the Earth ever be transformed into a moon, that is, become of the same significance, even if one is looking from the depths of space. They may appear in this way from a certain distance, but we all know that this is only appearance. We know this and do not get alarmed because we take it for granted that the reality of these things is fully accessible to us on the ground, not from a position in space. Hadjis, on the other hand, reverses this priority and makes appearance from space reality and reality on the ground mere appearance. In effect, he is saying that for all practical purposes – the purposes of everyday life – power is not to be taken more seriously than children's toys and that the Earth is no more significant than the Moon. This is surely a metaphysical claim, and the position in which Hadjis imagines himself beyond the world. To speak about this strange position, he is using the aeroplane and the Moon as convenient spatial metaphors.

In the second and third vignettes, the metaphysical nature of the position from which we all appear to be the Same begins to emerge more clearly. Even though he does not elaborate, Kazantzakis makes it plain that his Buddhist compassion for the world of struggle and division, his revelation that this world is 'Nothing' and the struggle absurd, is the outcome of 'complicated metaphysical reflection'. For their part, ordinary Cypriots reflect about the meaning of life and remember the fundamental equality of all people in the face of death. To this one may raise the objection, once again, that death is not a metaphysical phenomenon but as this-worldly and as empirical as anything else we know. Even though we do not experience our own death, we witness the death of others. This is no doubt true, but, as ethnographers know only too well, death always intimates something *beyond* itself. When we reflect on death, we do not merely think of it as an end – the end of life; we also conceptualise it as a passage – a passage through which, as the Cypriot saying has it, 'No one takes anything with him.' What lies on the other side of this passage could be anything that one cares to imagine. It could be, for example, another life, eternal or otherwise or, as in the case of Kazantzakis the atheist, an eternal darkness – nothingness. Whatever it might be, it makes little difference for the purposes of the present discussion. What is significant is that 'the other side' is imaginable and imagined. Indeed, it is necessarily so because there is no other way to speak about life in this way, that is, as an abstraction, without positing something other than life. In this sense, even nothingness is something and not nothing. It is an imaginary position, a metaphysical notion that we invent to reflect on, and talk about what is happening on 'this side'.

Having established that the position from which we all appear the Same is a metaphysical position, it is necessary to examine more closely what happens when one steps over to 'the other side'. To begin with, positioning oneself in the beyond makes it possible to constitute life, one's life as well as life in general, as a spectacle, as something to be primarily reflected upon rather than experienced and lived. This strange position has the effect of bringing into sharp focus what ordinary experience undoubtedly knows but only fleetingly, namely, life's limits, its beginning and end as well as what comes before and after; it directs attention away from life's content to the boundaries that contain it, and hence, by extension, to the boundlessness that surrounds both the content and the boundaries; and it compels those who occupy this strange position to contrast life with, measure it against, and evaluate it in relation to the infinity of the beyond. In short, in this strange position, what ordinary life knows but bypasses hurriedly becomes a glaring and inescapable fact: life is a radical finitude. With this comes another equally fundamental realisation, the revelation that in their finitude all human beings – whether rich or poor, important or unimportant, Western or Other – are essentially and fundamentally the Same. Despite these, and doubtless many other differences, all human beings emerge as indistinguishable little creatures, like Hadjis' ants, who struggle in the light for a moment and then perish.

It is human finitude, then, in its relation to the infinity of the beyond – be it God, Nothingness or the Great Unknown – that acts as the ultimate human equaliser. It is this relation that renders all differences utterly inconsequential and immaterial. For there is no human difference, irrespective of how enormous it might seem, that can even be compared with the absolute difference between the finite and the Infinite. Human differences – whether in terms of physical appearance, manners, practices or beliefs – make a difference only when they are measured by the standards of the here and now. Placed against the abyss that separates the finite and the Infinite, they are non-existent. Indeed, Sameness is exactly how human differences appear from the point of view of the Infinite that knows what it means to be finite.

There is little doubt that this is a powerful and highly persuasive image. Even though it is only visible from an imaginary position beyond the world and hence is itself imaginary, it appears as the very embodiment of reality and the truth. Indeed, the power of this image is so overwhelming that, as the three ethnographic vignettes demonstrate, it makes what is observable, concrete and tangible appear unreal and illusory. This is particularly pronounced in the case of Kazantzakis who sees life in general as little more than a 'spectacular illusion' – Nothingness. But it is also clear in the other two cases, especially in the way in which certain aspects of life are evaluated. For Hadjis, 'towers' and 'palaces' are not what they seem. No doubt, they appear imposing and mighty, but in 'reality' they are no more striking than children's toys. Ordinary Cypriots too – if only under certain circumstances – regard fame and power meaningless, the struggle to accumulate riches absurd and futile because, as they say, none of these things can be taken beyond the grave. Such notions are clearly at odds with the common-sense point of view, 'the earth- and time-bound notion of the world', as Mannheim (1936: 221) put it, which is primarily concerned with the domination of things and more often than not results also in the domination of people. From this point of view, far from being an illusion, wealth and power are precisely what make the world go round. And conversely, lack of wealth and power is what constrains people's lives in innumerable and often quite compelling ways.

Where, then, does the power of the vision of the world from a position beyond the world – of Sameness itself – come from? What is it that makes the 'unseen', as William James (1961) would say, and the metaphysical appear more realistic and factual than the empirical reality of the here and now? Let us return for a moment to the three ethnographic vignettes. In Hadjis's lyrics the organising theme is clearly pain and suffering. His friend is crying because she has been hurt by life's blows and Hadjis is asking her to stop taking what is causing her pain, and her pain itself seriously. In effect, he is telling her that there is another way of looking at the world, another way of being in the world – the only true way for Hadjis – which makes pain and suffering sufferable. Kazantzakis is clearly disturbed by the pettiness, greed and malice that he observes around him; but he is disturbed only for an instant. For he is certain that in the wider scheme of things – in reality – the struggle to gain advantage over others is for nothing. Indeed, he finds such comfort in this knowledge as to actually begin to feel compassion for all those who struggle thus and do not know what he does. Last, in the case of ordinary Cypriots and their comments in the face of death, what is at stake is social inequality and injustice. Some people are born rich and powerful, most are not so fortunate; some become rich and powerful by taking advantage of others, most are being taken advantage of. In the end, however – and at the end – such differences make no difference. Reflection on death and what comes after it restores, symbolically no doubt, the moral equilibrium of the world.

In all three cases, then, there is a certain denial of the world experience. This denial is not blind to the fact that pain and suffering, greed and malice, inequality and injustice exist in the world; what it refuses to accept rather is that such things are in any way 'real'. Although this attitude acknowledges that these profanities do indeed exist in the world, it flatly refuses to acknowledge that they are intrinsic to reality, an inescapable fact of the world. It is in this denial that the seductiveness of the image of the world from a position beyond the world, the power of the unseen and the metaphysical, is to be located. For what this denial does is nothing less than to render an otherwise unbearable world, a world of suffering and injustice, bearable and liveable. The world can now be borne and lived precisely because one is convinced that this is not at all what the 'real' world is about.

This brings me, at length, to the ethnographic 'vignettes' of the ethnographers themselves, to their attitude towards the world of experience, to what they deny in the same way, in the same sense and for the same reasons. Above anything else, there are two things in the world that do not belong to the world, according to ethnographers, two absurdities that should never be mistaken for what is 'real'. For ethnographers, the world's absurdities and unrealities *par excellence* are nothing other than racism and ethnocentrism; for them, the world that must be borne and lived is above all a racist and eth-nocentric world. If ethnographers persist in imagining, desiring and positing Sameness as a reality, then, it is because this metaphysical ontology of the human condition makes the world of experience – which is a world of division, inequality and injustice – bearable and liveable. It makes it so not by denying that racism and ethnocentrism exist in the world, but by denying that these profanities have anything to do with what the 'real' world is 'really' like.

With this, we have essentially arrived at the contemporary ethnological definition of magico-religious systems and at a very critical juncture. It is the point where what ethnographers say about Others, whether explicitly or otherwise, begins to turn in on itself and haunt them with vengeance. In the last chapter, I argued that both orthodox and heterodox anthropology, each in its own way, constructs a highly divisive image of the world. In this image Others emerge as those who require myths to protect themselves from the arbitrariness and meaninglessness of the world, while ethnographers appear as those who, in the spirit of the heroic thinking subject and for the sake of individual autonomy and freedom, refuse the support of such metaphysical crutches. In this chapter, having disenchanted Sameness thus far, it has become apparent that this image of the world is in need of radical modifica-tions. It now begins to look as though the heroic thinking subject may not be so daring after all, that there are certain domains of arbitrariness and meaninglessness in the world into which it would not venture without the support of the very Same metaphysical crutches it reserves for Others. The full extent to which ethnographers rely on Sameness to make their lives meaningful, however, can only become apparent though a more dynamic and diachronic analysis.

Anthropology flatly denies that the Otherness it encounters in the world is an intrinsic part of this world. In the process, it does not hesitate to reject itself whenever, which is always, it itself produces and reproduces Otherness – to reject itself either in part (this or that ethnological paradigm) or, as the case of heterodox discourse demonstrates, in whole. But this is a diachronic process; ethnological self-denials occur in time, over time and, as I will argue below, at the expense of time. The question, then, that I wish to raise in the following section is how the ethnological self-denial, and the denial of anthropology's time, compare with similar practices in the world that anthropology makes its object of study.

THE WILL TO MEANING

There is something quite remarkable about anthropology. It is a discipline without history. To say this is not to deny the obvious – that ethnological ideas began to proliferate with the discovery of the New World, that the time came when they were forged into a recognisable and recognised academic discipline and, that since then the discipline has evolved into numerous paradigms. Nor is it to deny what is equally obvious – that the story of these events, and the story of ethnological ideas associated with them have been recorded and are being transmitted, just like any other culture, to the younger generations of ethnographers. In this sense, anthropology does have a history. Yet this is a history which ethnographers themselves recognise only negatively as so many practices that took place under circumstances to be decried (for example, colonialism); and as so many discourses that reproduce, whether directly or otherwise, an impoverished myth – the myth that Western societies are culturally superior to the rest of the world. Anthropology, then, has no history because it is a story of the monumental failure to redeem Others, and as such a story, it is flatly rejected by the discipline's practitioners themselves.

It is hardly necessary to go into any detail here to show that such is, by and large, the ethnological evaluation of the discipline's history. It should suffice to state what has already been repeated several times in this book: first, that there is no ethnological paradigm – be it evolutionism, functionalism, structuralism or culturalism – that has not been found guilty, to a lesser or greater extent, for one reason or another, of the ultimate ethnological transgression – ethnocentrism; and, second, that the most recent ethnological paradigm, heterodox discourse, is a summary denial of the ethnocentric ethnological past and present, even of an anticipated ethnocentric future.

What is denied in the ethnological past is quite clear: it is racism and ethnocentrism. What it is for the sake of which this denial is effected is also quite clear: it is the reverse of racism and ethnocentrism, namely, Sameness. Put in this way, there is nothing remarkable either about what ethnographers deny or about what they affirm. Indeed, for most, these things go without saying – they do such things as a matter of course. Yet if what ethnographers deny and what they affirm do go without saying, it is only because they have forgotten (once again) to reflect on their beliefs and practices and to apply to themselves what they say about Others. Ethnographers certainly find it worthy of reflection and analysis that Others deny the passage of time, that they attempt, as it is often claimed, to protect cultural categories and systems of classification from the erosion that time brings. For a discipline that denies its own history this interest in the Other's denial of time is highly ironic, to say the least. But perhaps one can use the exhaustive ethnological analyses as a rough guide in explaining why ethnographers themselves deny their own past. I propose to turn first to a recent attempt to reflect on, and analyse the time of the Other, Sahlins's theory of historical change or lack thereof. I shall then try to reverse the flow of discourse and channel it back to its source.

Let me begin with a quotation. 'If culture is as anthropologists claim a meaningful order', Sahlins points out:

still, in action meanings are always at risk. They are risked, for example, by reference to things (i.e., in extension). Things not only have their own *raison d'être*, independently of what people make of them, they are inevitably disproportionate to the sense of the signs by which they are apprehended ... Culture is therefore a gamble with nature, in the course of which ... the old names that are still on everyone's lips acquire connotations that are far removed from their original meaning. This is one of the historical processes that I will call 'the functional revaluation of the categories'. (1985: ix)

The risk that Sahlins sees in action is none other than the possible conflict between cultural categories and the empirical world. The latter always escapes human attempts to frame it conceptually, and this means that cultural categories put into practice are likely to be contradicted by empirical reality. What happens next is the key to historical change. 'In the contradictory encounters with persons and things, signs are liable to be reclaimed by the original powers of their creation: the human symbolic consciousness.' If they are reclaimed, their meaning is transformed – 'functionally revaluated', in Sahlins's jargon – which in turn leads to change. The categories now mean something new, and new meanings lead to new things. If the categories are not reclaimed and transformed, if one finds fault with the empirical world rather than with one's 'signs', there is no change; the categories are maintained and, as Mary Douglas has shown, the things of the empirical world that contradict them are designated as dirt and are avoided – they become 'pollution and taboo'.

While Douglas flatly refuses to distinguish between 'us' and 'them' when it comes to the protection of cultural categories from the empirical world, Sahlins argues that the West no longer engages in such defensive practices. It is only 'the Rest' that do so. As he points out, cultural categories are subjected to empirical risks and historical change becomes possible only 'to the extent that people, as they are socially enabled, cease to be slaves of their concepts and become the masters' (1985: x). Not all people, however, are thus socially enabled, according to Sahlins. In some societies, such as the Polynesian cultures that he studied, people are 'slaves' to their ideas – or were until taught differently by colonialism. For Sahlins, then, there is an important distinction to be made between the Other's 'mytho-praxis' – practices that refuse to come to terms with the realities of the empirical world and hence lead nowhere – and 'the disenchanted utilitarianism of our historical consciousness' that takes us everywhere (1985: xi). Is this really the case, or is Sahlins leading us, and himself, astray?

It is ironic that Sahlins speaks with such certainty, not to say arrogance, about 'our disenchanted' consciousness. Sameness, the most fundamental ethnological category, what is nearest and to most ethnographers dearest, can hardly be called a disenchanted and utilitarian concept; and it certainly is not an object of a *historical* consciousness. If what has been argued in this book has any truth to it, Sameness runs no empirical risks at all in ethnological hands; indeed, it could not be safer. But this is not because ethnographers do not 'gamble' with the empirical world – they do so every day in the field. Nor is it because, when Sameness is 'extended' it fits with what ethnographers see around them; on the contrary, its encounters are always contradictory. Rather, Sameness runs no risks because it is *never* 'reclaimed' by ethnological consciousness, *never* 'functionally revaluated'. Whenever Sameness is in conflict with 'persons and things', which is always, ethnographers find fault with reality – persons and things, they say, are racist and ethnocentric. This means, among other things, that since E.B. Tylor's time, Sameness has been placed in a strange region beyond the reach of the empirical world and remains completely unaffected by all those ethnological (and non-ethnological) discourses and practices that contradict and undermine it. It means that, for the last 150 years, ethnographers have placed and maintained Sameness outside the 'disenchanted utilitarianism' of their 'historical consciousness' – on the other side of time and history. With this, we are once again in the domain of the religious and the metaphysical or, as Sahlins would say, the world of 'mytho-praxis'. But this time, it is the ethnographer's own world we are dealing with.

To explore further the ethnological practice of denying time for the sake of Sameness, the desire to insulate it from the vicissitudes of time and history, I shall turn to Mircea Eliade and his small but important book, *Cosmos and History* (1959). Eliade's theme is 'primitive' and 'archaic' societies' denial of history, a denial motivated by what one might call 'a will to meaning'. One of the book's main arguments is that, by adopting the 'primitive' attitude towards time, Western 'man' will be able to avoid despair – the despair that befalls cultures in which life in general, and suffering in particular, have no meaning outside themselves. Apparently Eliade assumes that Western 'man', or at least the educated elite among Western 'men', have long lost touch with this 'primitive' attitude and has become thoroughly historicist. If the foregoing discussion has any truth to it, however, it should be apparent that ethnographers, if not anyone else in the West, are not the kind of 'men' that Eliade has in mind.

Even though 'primitive' and 'archaic' societies are 'conscious of a certain form of history', writes Eliade (1959: xi), they 'make every effort to disregard it'. Indeed, for Eliade, the most fundamental characteristic of such societies is 'their revolt against concrete, historical time, their nostalgia for a periodical return to the mythical beginning of things, to the "Great Time"'. This theme is well-known to ethnographers. Lévi-Strauss (1966: 232) too finds that there is a 'fundamental antipathy' towards history in native societies, but his explanation of this phenomenon, particularly in *The Savage Mind*, veers away from the direction that I wish to follow here. For Lévi-Strauss, this 'antipathy' has to do mainly with cognitive considerations, namely, the kind of classifications that the 'savage mind' constructs and the dangers that history poses to them. Such cognitive considerations cannot easily be dissociated from existential questions, however, and indeed, overall, Lévi-Strauss makes no such attempt. Elsewhere, for example, he places the emphasis on meaning rather than on cognition (cf. 1963). What is often implicit in Lévi-Strauss becomes the primary point of reference in Eliade's work. For him, native depreciation of history reflects rejection of the profane in human affairs – of the absurd and meaningless – and signifies celebration of the sacred. In this practice, Eliade (1959: xi) detects 'a certain metaphysical "valorization" of human existence' itself.

'Primitive' societies valorise human existence, Eliade argues, because they refuse to accord everyday practices autonomous and intrinsic value. They acquire value, 'and in so doing become real', that is, meaningful, 'because they participate after one fashion or another, in a reality that transcends them' (1959: 4). There are three ways in which natives depreciate everyday practices, according to Eliade, three strategies they employ to deny intrinsic significance to historical events. First, they strive to imitate exemplary models of behaviour – what Eliade calls 'archetypes' – be it the life of gods or mythical ancestors and heroes. Insofar as they succeed in this endeavour, they effectively remain outside history and the profanity of everyday life. They act in a manner that has been consecrated by gods and ancestors at the beginning of time which means that they permanently sojourn in this beginning. Alternatively, natives seek to regenerate time periodically, to return, that is, to the beginning of time and participate in the cosmological act of the world's Creation. The effect of this symbolic return is effacement of all the profanities that have occurred during the course of ordinary life and hence purification, rebirth, a new beginning. In yet another strategy, ordinary human existence is imbued with metahistorical significance. Everyday life and its hardships become meaningful and hence bearable because they are now seen as a necessary step towards the end of time and salvation. All these practices, Eliade argues, reflect a wish 'not to lose contact with *being*' (1959: 92), a desire to stay as close as possible to 'the heart of the *real*' (1959: 95), a will to a meaningful existence.

There is really no doubt that the ethnological culture valorises human existence as much as 'primitive' and 'archaic' societies. But nor should there be any doubt either about the metaphysical status of the ethnological valorisation. Sameness is a conception of the world from an imaginary position beyond the world. Indeed, on the basis of Eliade's typology, it is now possible to provide a more precise description of its transcendental nature. Let us, then, first say that Sameness refers to the 'Great Time' at the beginning of time before the fall from grace. During this remarkable time innocence was still the order of the world, the evils of division and difference – of racism and ethnocentrism – had not yet appeared and human beings existed in a blissful state of unity and oneness – a state of human purity and pure humanity. Let us also point out that Sameness functions very much like what Eliade calls an 'archetype'. There is no need for ethnographers to regenerate time and to return to the 'Great Time' periodically. Nor is there any need for them to posit the Beginning at the end of time – to imbue life, that is, with metahistorical significance. There is no such need because ethnographers sojourn permanently in the Beginning. As far as they are concerned, Sameness is right here, right now, and has never left us. Sameness *is* reality. No doubt, the ethnographer would argue, there are many people who do not perceive this reality, but this is hardly because Sameness does not exist. Rather it is because such people are blind to it, or ignorant or, worse still, evil.

Because ethnographers strive to remain permanently in the 'Great Time', because they struggle to be in constant 'contact with being' and as close as possible to 'the heart of the real', because, in short, they will a meaningful existence, they must deny history and the profanities that it brings about – and they do. Ethnographers do not hesitate to denounce anything that contradicts and undermines Sameness, any manifestation of racism and ethnocentrism, including those manifestations that they encounter in their own discursive practices, past or present. Hence the fact that anthropology is a discipline without history or, at any rate, a discipline with a history denied.

At the beginning of this chapter, I raised the question as to why ethnographers are unable to demonstrate what they posit as the only real reality of the world, namely, Sameness. I argued that this is so because Sameness is impossible, and that it is impossible because ethnographers are caught in the double bind of trying to be both the Creators of a world of Sameness and creatures in the world they themselves have created. I also argued that, despite the impossibility of demonstrating Sameness, ethnographers must nonetheless persist in their Sisyphian efforts. It should now be apparent why this must be the case. Ethnological discourse and practice are driven by an implacable force, a certain will that wills what can never be. This is not Nietzsche's 'will to power'; on the contrary, it is a will that strives to eradicate all power. Nor is it Foucault's more sophisticated version of it – a will to knowledge and the truth. There can be no will to knowledge, the truth or anything else for that matter in an absurd and senseless world. What drives ethnographers to produce knowledge and uphold what they posit as the truth is a powerful desire for a symbolically unified and hence ethically meaningful world. It is, in short, a will to meaning.

AT THE END OF THE GAME

At the end of this exploration of the ethnological imagination, its hidden desires and longings, what it thinks it knows about Others and flaunts but also what it cannot imagine about itself and must remain oblivious to, it is time to pause and take stock. It is time not only to summarise what has been said so far but also to examine what it all means and to explore its implications for all those involved in the anthropological drama – in the first place, all those whom anthropology has long turned into 'natives' and, second but equally important, those who are anthropology's true natives, namely, its own practitioners.

Let me begin by outlining the main points of the argument. First, and contrary to what heterodox discourse maintains, there has never been a crisis in ethnological representation. No such crisis has ever existed because the truth of the most fundamental ethnological representation – Sameness – is questioned by no one, heterodox ethnographers included. Second, whatever else anthropology might be about, it has always been, primarily and fundamentally, a persistent and uncompromising attempt to demonstrate what ethnographers know and posit as the truth of the world. The redemptive strategies of orthodox anthropology are testimony to this, and so is the most recent, heterodox strategy which reduces the problem of Otherness to a purely epistemological problem and attempts to smuggle what is meta-epistemological about the discipline – Sameness – through the back door. Third, the struggle to demonstrate Sameness has never been, and can never be won. Ironically, ethnographers have always been their worst enemies. There is no ethnological paradigm that has not been found guilty of ethnocentrism, not a single one that has not produced an image of the world in which the West confronts the Other as a superior sociocultural universe. As I have shown in this study, one of the primary ways in which this division is effected is through the positing of a native unconscious – a sociocultural ignorance. Fourth, the historical failure of ethnographers to achieve what they imagine and desire reflects a fundamental ontological problem. Sameness is impossible because ethnographers are caught in the ontological double bind of trying to be both subjects and objects, both the creators of a world of Sameness and creatures in the world they have created. Finally, ethnographers must persist in this self-defeating exercise because giving up Sameness would mean giving up the struggle against racism and ethnocentrism. Ethnographers cannot bear racism and ethnocentrism because they cannot bear an ethically absurd, arbitrary and meaningless world. They too require the support of softening myths and comforting illusions.

The end of this exploration, then, reveals a vicious ontological circle: every attempt to demonstrate Sameness inevitably results in the production of Otherness; every manifestation of Otherness must sooner or later be reckoned and dealt with; every attempt to deal with Otherness can do nothing more than to reproduce it further down the road. Such is the internal dynamic of the discipline, the mechanism responsible for the proliferation of ethnological discourse, a will to produce knowledge that would sustain the 'truth' which is driven by a will to meaning.

The end of this exploration is also the end of an agonistic academic performance which is inspired by the ethos and 'unauthorised' practices of Cypriot and Cretan highlanders. I cannot know what they – and Others like and unlike them – would make of it, whether they would think of it as a performance that 'says something' and has *simasia* (meaning). Nor can I know whether it would make them laugh at the grandiose claims of the powers that I have been dealing with. This has certainly been my aim. Ethnographers claim to be authorities on knowledge. They claim to know fundamental things about native life which the natives whose life it is allegedly do not know. More recently, ethnographers claim to have discovered fundamental things about themselves as well. In this study I have shown that what they claim to know is facile and spurious because they are oblivious to what is truly fundamental – what drives them to know to begin with, the condition of possibility of anything ethnological that they could possibly imagine about themselves and Others. It remains hidden and constitutes an unconscious in its own right – the ethnological unthought. There is a biting irony in all this. The self-proclaimed authorities on knowledge 'don't know' and must remain ignorant of what makes possible what they know. If this is not farcical enough to make natives laugh, perhaps it can produce an amused native smile.

As for the true natives of anthropology, the ethnographers themselves, all that remains to be said to them at the end of the game is what is usually being said in such circumstances: 'It's been a really good game; if you want to play again, don't hesitate to ask.'

NOTES

1   INTRODUCTION: OF SCHOLARS, GAMBLERS AND THIEVES

1. This book develops ideas that first appeared in Argyrou (1999).
2. What follows draws on my review of Chakrabarty's book (Argyrou, 2001).
3. See, for example, Argyrou (1996b, 1997).
4. Because much of this discussion on agonistic displays is concerned with the practices of men, it may appear that this is strictly a masculine ethos. As Herzfeld (1991) and Dubisch (1995) have shown however, this is not quite true. Women may act in different ways but their actions are often as agonistic as the actions of men. It is true however that a full account of such female practices remains to be written.

2   HAS THERE EVER BEEN A CRISIS IN ETHNOLOGICAL REPRESENTATION

1. Although they draw radically different conclusions from Foucault, two of the best-known contemporary social theorists, Giddens (1990) and Beck (1992), make 'reflexivity,' both in the social and intellectual realms, the very essence of modernity. Giddens, for example, argues that 'what is characteristic of modernity is not an embracing of the new for its own sake, but the presumption of wholesale reflexivity – which of course includes reflection upon the nature of reflection itself' (1990: 39).
2. Clifford (1988d), for example, argues that Said often lapses into a rather un-Foucaultian 'humanism'. On the connections between Said's postcolonial critique and 'postmodernity' see Moore-Gilbert (1997) and Gandhi (1998).
3. Feminist ethnographers recognise this themselves. Di Leonardo (1991: 1–2), for example, points out that while twenty years ago 'Western feminist scholars ... had a sharp, taken-for-granted starting point', today they recognise 'both the adjective of location – we are *Western* feminists, and there are others – and the noun's contingent, historically determined existence'.
4. Such dismissals are by now a commonplace and come from both a Marxist, 'materialist' perspective and non-Marxist ones. For a representative example of the former see Polier and Roseberry (1989); for a dismissal of heterodox discourse from the perspective of positive social science see D'Andrade (1995).
5. It should be pointed out, however, that Foucault does not escape a similar paradox – ironically, the very paradox that he located in the work of others – in his earlier work on the human sciences. For an extended discussion of this issue see Dreyfus and Rabinow (1982: 79–103).
6. See, for instance, the work of Pagden (1982) on Christian ethnology. See also Stocking (1982 [1968], 1987).
7. Quoted in Tylor (1874: 418). See also Morris (1987: 91).
8. For a discussion of Boas's contribution to the pluralisation of the notion of culture see Stocking (1982 [1968]).

9. Critiques of individual paradigms abound. For a truly comprehensive one, a critique that encompasses all major ethnological paradigms from evolutionism to culturalism, see Fabian (1983).

3 THE SALVATION INTENT

1. This, of course, is a simplification of the much more complex encounter between the Hawaiians and Captain Cook. Nonetheless, it captures the essence of Sahlins' argument.
2. For a fuller treatment of this example see Argyrou (1996a).
3. For a classic ethnological example see Taussig's (1980) famous book on Colombian peasants and Bolivian miners. For an equally classic work from the economic historian's perspective see Polanyi (1944).
4. For a similar, and earlier, attempt see Parry and Bloch (1989).
5. Margaret Hodgen (1966) traces the origin of ethnology to Herodotus, but this practice must be placed within the broader Eurocentric tradition that constituted classical Greece as the cradle of Western civilisation (cf. Herzfeld 1987; Bernal 1987). The discussion on the Spanish churchmen that follows draws on Pagden's (1982) excellent study.
6. Tylor, according to Stocking, resigned his membership of the London Ethnological Society because he could not tolerate the racism of this society's president.
7. For an extensive discussion on this issue see Tambiah (1990: 20–4).
8. Quoted in Morris (1987: 91).
9. Tylor employed the term 'race' to refer to what we would call peoples or cultures rather than to distinct biological groups. For a discussion of the uses of the term in evolutionist thought see Stocking (1982: 110–32).
10. These ideas were subsequently developed by Frazer (1963 [1922]) and given expression in the well-known distinction between two types of magic, 'imitative' and 'contagious'.
11. It is ironic perhaps, but certainly instructive that more than a century after Tylor, anthropology, in its heterodox guise, would return to the notion of the 'poetic' to make a similar argument, this time about itself (see Clifford and Marcus 1986). I discuss this issue in greater detail in the next chapter.
12. Even though she criticises Durkheim for postulating a unified society, Douglas falls into the same trap herself. She fails to see that not everyone within the same society shares the same systems of classification and hence that what is dirt for some individuals and social groups may not be for others. For a detailed exposition of this argument see Argyrou (1997).
13. Geertz does not explicitly state this, but it is implied in his use of Evans-Pritchard's work on Zande witchcraft. It is also implicit in the way he appropriates Max Weber's (1946a) work. The latter associates the problem of suffering with magic and the problem of injustice with religion. Significantly enough, Geertz does not feel the need to make such a distinction.
14. For a quasi-formal but enlightening debate, the reader is referred to the 1995 and 1996 issues of the *Anthropology Newsletter*.

4 WHAT THE NATIVES DON'T KNOW

1. For a recent discussion on another miraculous icon of the Virgin on the Greek island of Tinos see Dubisch (1995).
2. It could be argued, of course, that redundancy is necessary if the message is to be convincing. Sperber is aware of this argument but he dismisses it rather hastily. As he points out, 'redundancy alone creates lassitude more than conviction' (1975: 8).

3. In his discussion of omens, Tylor (1874: 120) argues that 'anyone who takes the trouble to go into the subject in detail ... will discover that the principle of direct symbolism still accounts for a fair proportion of them'.
4. On the sacred nature of native myths see Eliade's (1959) classic study.
5. Both quoted by Douglas (1966), pages 71 and 72 respectively.
6. I am following Geertz's (1973a) own example here, which distinguishes between two different kinds of dam-builders – the beaver and the engineer.
7. See, for instance, Clifford (1988a) and Tyler (1986).
8. A classic example would be the Christian existentialist thinker Søren Kierkegaard. See in particular his views on the question of doubt (1985 [1844]).
9. Thus, in the classic dichotomy, the three elements that I have identified as being constitutive of the modern subject – thinking, autonomy and daring – are identified with men, while their opposites – emotion, dependence and passivity – with women.
10. I owe this significant insight to Nancy Ries.

5   THE ETHNOLOGICAL WILL TO MEANING

1. In his *Critique of Pure Reason* (1934 [1781]), Kant has shown that time is nothing – not a being in the world. It is, rather, one of the modes – the other being space – in which human beings apprehend Being. Kant's argument was anticipated by Saint Augustine in his *Confessions* (1912 [1631]) where he argues that time is nothing other than the human consciousness remembering the past and anticipating the future by making things present to itself.
2. For Lévy-Bruhl, as for Durkheim, the conditions of possibility of self-consciousness and knowledge are social, not psychological. This becomes quite clear in the last chapter of Lévy-Bruhl's (1925) book, and shows that, as Evans-Pritchard (1965) himself pointed out, he was not a racist.
3. Sartre uses the term 'Other' to refer to anyone other than the self. To avoid confusion with the ethnological Other, I will be referring to Sartre's term as 'other'.
4. In the *Phenomenology of Spirit*, Hegel (1977 [1807]) breaks this cognitive process into three steps. The first is 'sense-certainty' where the subject merely confronts an object, that is, becomes aware of it as object. The second is 'perception' where the subject begins to distinguish the object's properties; and the third is 'understanding' where the object, now fully grasped, is placed in a wider conceptual scheme. 'Sense-perception' approximates what Sartre has in mind with the notion of ontological separation.
5. For an extended discussion of middle-class strategies of distinction in Cyprus as well as the opposition's response to them see Argyrou (1996b, 1997).
6. I have argued elsewhere (Argyrou 1996b) that the Cypriot elite's claims to a European identity are denied in at least two ways. The first depicts Cypriot modernity as an imitation of the original European modernity and the second as a loss of the 'traditional', 'authentic' Cypriot identity.
7. See, for example, Comaroff (1985) and Escobar (1995). See also Scott (1985).
8. The book is known in English as 'Zorba the Greek' after the title of the film by Mikhalis Cacoyiannis that made the book known in the English-speaking world. The translation that follows is mine.
9. The literature on male honour and female shame or sexual modesty in the Mediterranean region is vast. One should mention perhaps the pioneering volume of essays edited by Peristiany (1965) and a more recent volume edited by Gilmore (1987). For critical responses see especially Herzfeld (1980, 1987) and Pina-Cabral (1989).
10. On the often brutal imagery of death in Greek laments see Danforth (1982).

REFERENCES

Argyrou, Vassos. 1993. Under a spell: the strategic use of magic in Greek Cypriot Society. *American Ethnologist* 20: 259–71.

—— 1996a. Is 'closer and closer' ever close enough? De-reification, diacritical power, and the specter of evolutionism. *Anthropological Quarterly* 69: 206–19.

—— 1996b. *Tradition and Modernity in the Mediterranean: The Wedding as Symbolic Struggle.* Cambridge: Cambridge University Press.

—— 1997. 'Keep Cyprus clean': littering, pollution, and otherness. *Cultural Anthropology* 12: 159–78.

—— 1999. Sameness and the ethnological will to meaning. *Current Anthropology* 40: S29–S41.

—— 2001. 'Provincializing Europe': reflections on questions of method and strategy. *Social Anthropology* 9: 217–22.

Asad, Talal. 1993. *Genealogies of Religion: Discipline and Reasons of Power in Christianity and Islam.* Baltimore, MD: Johns Hopkins University Press.

Augustine, Saint. 1912 [1631]. *Confessions.* London: Heinemann.

Beck, Ulrich. 1992. *Risk and Society: Towards a New Modernity.* London: Sage.

Bernal, Martin. 1987 *Black Athena: The Afroasiatic Roots of Classical Civilization.* New Brunswick: Rutgers University Press.

Bourdieu, Pierre. 1977. *Outline of a Theory of Practice.* Cambridge: Cambridge University Press.

—— 1984. *Distinction: A Social Critique of the Judgement of Taste.* Cambridge, MA: Harvard University Press.

Carrier, James. 1992. Occidentalism: the world turned upside-down. *American Ethnologist* 19: 195–212.

—— 1995. (ed.) *Occidentalism: Images of the West.* Oxford: Oxford University Press.

Chakrabarty, Dipesh. 2000. *Provincializing Europe: Postcolonial Thought and Historical Difference.* Princeton, NJ: Princeton University Press.

Clifford, James. 1986a. Introduction: partial truths. In *Writing Culture: The Poetics and Politics of Ethnography,* James Clifford and George Marcus (eds). Berkeley: University of California Press.

—— 1986b. On ethnographic allegory. In *Writing Culture, The Poetics and Politics of Ethnography,* James Clifford and George Marcus (eds). Berkely: University of California Press.

—— 1988a. Introduction: the pure products go crazy. In *The Predicament of Culture: Twentieth-century Ethnography, Literature, and Art.* Cambridge, MA: Harvard University Press.

—— 1988b. On ethnographic authority. In *The Predicament of Culture: Twentieth-century Ethnography, Literature and Art.* Cambridge MA: Harvard University Press.

—— 1988c. On Ethnographic Self-fashioning. In *The Predicament of Culture: Twentieth-century Ethnography, Literature and Art.* Cambridge MA: Harvard University Press.

—— 1988d. On Orientalism. In *The Predicament of Culture: Twentieth-century Ethnography, Literature and Art.* Cambridge MA: Harvard University Press.

Clifford, James and George Marcus (eds). 1986. *Writing Culture; The Poetics and Politics of Ethnography.* Berkeley: University of California Press.

Cyprus News Agency. 1997a. Weeping icon moves a nation. www.cyna.org.cy
    7 February: 2–4.
—— 1997b. Thousands attend prayer at Kykko monastery. www.cyna.org.cy
    9 February: 2.
Comaroff, Jean. 1985. *Body of Power, Spirit of Resistance*. Chicago: University of Chicago
    Press.
Crapanzano, Vincent. 1986. Hermes' dilemma: the masking of subversion in ethnographic
    description. In *Writing Culture: The Poetics and Politics of Ethnography*. James Clifford and
    George Marcus (eds). Berkeley: University of California Press.
D'Andrade, Roy. 1995. Objectivity and militancy. *Current Anthropology* 36 (3): 399–408.
Danforth, Loring. 1982. *The Death Rituals of Rural Greece*. Princeton, NJ: Princeton
    University Press.
Derrida, Jacques. 1992. *Given Time: I. Counterfeit Money*. Chicago: University of Chicago
    Press.
Di Leonardo, Micaela. (ed.) 1991. *Gender at the Crossroads of Knowledge*. Berkeley: University
    of California Press.
Douglas, Mary. 1966. *Purity and Danger: An Analysis of the Concepts of Pollution and Taboo*.
    London: Routledge.
Dreyfus, Hubert, and Paul Rabinow. 1982. *Michel Foucault: Beyond Structuralism and
    Hermeneutics*. Chicago: University of Chicago Press.
Dubisch, Jill. 1995. *In a Different Place: Pilgrimage, Gender, and Politics at a Greek Island Shrine*.
    Princeton, NJ: Princeton University Press.
Durkheim, Emile. 1976 [1915]. *The Elementary Forms of the Religious Life*. London: George
    Allen and Unwin.
Eliade, Mircea. 1959. *Cosmos and History: The Myth of Eternal Return*. New York: Harper
    and Row.
Escobar, Arturo. 1995. *Encountering Development: The Making and Unmaking of the Third
    World*. Princeton, NJ: Princeton University Press.
Evans-Pritchard, E.E. 1965. *Theories of Primitive Religion*. Oxford: Clarendon Press.
—— 1976 [1937]. *Witchcraft, Oracles, and Magic among the Azande*. Abridged and
    Introduced by Eva Gillies. Oxford: Clarendon Press.
Fabian, Johannes. 1983. *Time and the Other: How Anthropology Makes its Object*. New York:
    Columbia University Press.
Foucault, Michel. 1970. *The Order of Things: An Archaeology of the Human Sciences*. New
    York: Vintage.
—— 1979. *Discipline and Punish: The Birth of the Prison*. New York: Vintage.
—— 1984. What is Enlightment? In *The Foucault Reader*, Paul Rabinow (ed.). Har-
    mondsworth: Penguin.
Frazer, Sir James. 1963 [1922]. *The Golden Bough*. New York: Collier.
Gandhi, Leela. 1998. *Postcolonial Theory: A Critical Introduction*. Edinburgh: Edinburgh
    University Press.
Geertz, Clifford. 1973a. The impact of the concept of culture on the concept of man. In *The
    Interpretation of Cultures*. New York: Basic Books.
—— 1973b. Religion as a cultural system. In *The Interpretation of Cultures*. New York: Basic
    Books.
—— 1983. 'From the native's point of view: on the nature of anthropological under-
    standing. In *Local Knowledge*, pp. 55–70. London: Fontana.
—— 1988. *Works and Lives: The Anthropologist as Author*. Stanford, CA: Stanford University
    Press.
Giddens, Anthony. 1990. *The Consequences of Modernity*. Stanford, CA: Stanford University
    Press.
Gilmore, David (ed.). 1987. *Honor and Shame and the Unity of the Mediterranean*.
    Washington, DC: American Anthropological Association, Special Publication no. 22.

Habermas, Jürgen. 1994. Some questions concerning the theory of power: Foucault again. In *Critique of Power: Recasting the Foucault/Habermas Debate*, Michael Kelly (ed.). Cambridge, MA: MIT Press.

Hegel, G.W.F. 1977 [1807]. *Phenomenology of Spirit*. Oxford: Oxford University Press.

Heidegger, Martin. 1977a. What is metaphysics? In *Basic Writings*, David Farrell Krell (ed.). San Francisco: HarperCollins.

—— 1977b. *The Question Concerning Technology and Other Essays*. New York: Harper and Row.

—— 1996 [1926]. *Being and Time*. New York: SUNY Press.

Herzfeld, Michael. 1980. Honour and shame: problems in the comparative analysis of moral systems. *Man* (ns) 15: 339–51.

—— 1985. *The Poetics of Manhood: Contest and Identity in a Cretan Mountain Village*. Princeton, NJ: Princeton University Press.

—— 1987. *Anthropology through the Looking-Glass: Critical Ethnography in the Margins of Europe*. Cambridge: Cambridge University Press.

—— 1991. Silence, submission, and subversion: toward a poetics of womanhood. In *Contested Identities: Gender and Kinship in Modern Greece*, Peter Loizos and E. Papataxiarchis (eds). Princeton, NJ: Princeton University Press.

Hodgen, Margaret. 1966. *Early Anthropology in the Sixteenth and Seventeenth Centuries*. Philadelphia, PA: University of Pennsylvania Press.

Hume, David. 1977 [1748]. *An Enquiry Concerning Human Understanding*. Indianapolis: Hackett.

James, William. 1961. *The Varieties of Religious Experience*. New York: Macmillan.

Kant, Immanuel. 1934 [1781]. *Critique of Pure Reason*. London: Everyman's Library.

—— 1970a [1784]. An answer to the question: 'What is Enlightenment?' In *Kant: Political Writings*, Hans Reiss and H.B. Nisbet (eds). Cambridge: Cambridge University Press.

—— 1970b [1786]. What is orientation in thinking? In *Kant: Political Writingss*, Hans Reiss and H.B. Nisbet (eds). Cambridge: Cambridge University Press.

Kazantzakis, Nikos. 1973. *O Vios ki i Politia tou Alexi Zorba* (The Life and Times of Alexi Zorba). Athens: El. Kazantzaki.

Kierkegaard, Søren. 1985 [1844]. *Philosophical Fragments/Johannes Climacus*, Howard V. Hong and Edna H. Hong (eds). Princeton, NJ: Princeton University Press.

Kuklick, Henrica. 1991. *The Savage Within: The Social History of British Anthropology, 1885–1945*. Cambridge: Cambridge University Press.

Las Casas, Bartolome de. 1992 [1542]. *A Short Account of the Destruction of the Indies*. Harmondsworth: Penguin.

Lévi-Strauss, Claude. 1963. The effectiveness of symbols. In *Structural Anthropology 1*. Harmondsworth: Penguin.

—— 1966. *The Savage Mind*. Chicago: University of Chicago Press.

—— 1969. *The Raw and the Cooked*. Chicago: The University of Chicago Press.

—— 1973. *Tristes tropiques*. Harmondsworth: Penguin.

Lévy-Bruhl, Lucien. 1925. *How Natives Think*. New York: Knopf.

Lovejoy, Arthur. 1936. *The Great Chain of Being*. Cambridge, MA: Harvard University Press.

Malinowski, Bronislaw. 1922. *The Argonauts of the Western Pacific*. Prospect Heights, IL: Waveland.

—— 1948 [1925]. *Magic, Science and Religion*. New York: Doubleday.

Mannheim, Karl. 1936. *Ideology and Utopia*. San Diego: Harcourt Brace.

Marcus, George, and Michael Fischer. 1986. *Anthropology as Cultural Critique*. Chicago: University of Chicago Press.

Mauss, Marcel. 1967 [1925]. *The Gift: Forms and Functions of Exchange in Archaic Societies*. New York: Norton.

Mead, Margaret. 1930. *Growing Up in New Guinea*. Harmondsworth: Penguin.

Metcalf, Peter. 1978. Death be not strange. *Natural History* 87: 6–12.

Moore-Gilbert, Bart. 1997. *Postcolonial Theory: Contexts, Practices, Politics*. London: Verso.

Morris, Brian. 1987. *Anthropological Studies of Religion*. Cambridge: Cambridge University Press.

Obeyesekere, Gananath. 1992. *The Apotheosis of Captain Cook: European Mythmaking in the Pacific*. Princeton, NJ: Princeton University Press.

Ong, Aihwa. 1987. *Spirits of Resistance and Capitalist Discipline: Factory Women in Malaysia*. New York: SUNY Press.

Orwell, George. 1949. *Nineteen Eighty-Four*. Harmondsworth: Penguin.

Pagden, Anthony. 1982. *The Fall of Natural Man: The American Indian and the Origins of Comparative Ethnology*. Cambridge: Cambridge University Press.

Parry, Jonathan. 1989. On the moral perils of exchange. In *Money and the Morality of Exchange*, Jonathan Parry and Maurice Bloch (eds.). Cambridge: Cambridge University Press.

Parry, Jonathan, and Maurice Bloch (eds.) 1989. *Money and the Morality of Exchange*. Cambridge: Cambridge University Press.

Peristiany, J. G. 1965. Honour and shame in a Cypriot highland village. In *Honour and Shame: The Values of Mediterranean Society*, J.G. Peristiany (ed.). London: Weidenfeld and Nicolson.

Pina-Cabral, João de. 1989. The Mediterranean as a category of regional comparison: a critical view. *Current anthropology* 30: 399–406.

Polanyi, Karl. 1944 *The Great Transformation: The Political and Economic Crisis of Our Time*. Boston: Beacon Press.

Polier, Nicole and William Roseberry. 1989. Tristes tropes: post-modern anthropologists encounter the other and discover themselves. *Economy and Society* 18: 245–64.

Rosaldo, Renato. 1986. From the door of his tent: the fieldworker and the inquisitor. In *Writing Culture: The Poetics and Politics of Ethnography*, James Clifford and George Marcus (eds.). Berkeley: University of California Press.

Sahlins, Marshall. 1977. *Culture and Practical Reason*. Chicago: University of Chicago Press.

—— 1985. *Islands in History*. Chicago: University of Chicago Press.

—— 1995. *How Natives Think, about Captain Cook for Example*. Chicago: University of Chicago Press.

Said, Edward. 1978. *Orientalism*. New York: Vintage.

Sartre, Jean-Paul. 1958 [1943]. *Being and Nothingness*. London: Routledge.

Scott, James. 1985. *Weapons of the Weak: Everyday Forms of Peasant Resistance*. New Haven, CT: Yale University Press.

Sperber, Dan. 1975. *Rethinking Symbolism*. Cambridge: Cambridge University Press.

Stocking, George. 1982 [1968]. *Race, Culture and Evolution: Essays in the History of Anthropology*. Chicago: University of Chicago Press.

—— 1987. *Victorian Anthropology*. Boston, MA: Free Press.

Tambiah, Stanley. 1990. *Magic, Science, Religion, and the Scope of Rationality*. Cambridge: Cambridge University Press.

Taussig, Michael. 1980. *The Devil and Commodity Fetishism in South America*. Chapel Hill, NC: University of North Carolina Press.

Tyler, Stephen. 1986. Post-modern ethnography: from document of the occult to occult document. In *Writing Culture: The Poetics and Politics of Ethnography*, James Clifford and George Marcus (eds). Berkeley: University of California Press.

Tylor, Edward. 1874. *Primitive Culture*, Volume 1. New York: Henry Holt.

Weber, Max. 1946a. The social psychology of the world religions. In *From Max Weber*, H.H. Gerth and C. Wright Mills (eds). New York: Oxford University Press.

—— 1946b. Science as a vocation. In *From Max Weber*, H.H. Gerth and C. Wright Mills (eds). New York: Oxford University Press.

—— 1946c. Religious rejections of the world and their directions. In *From Max Weber*, H.H. Gerth and C. Wright Mills (eds). New York: Oxford University Press.

Weiner, Annette. 1988. *The Trobrianders of Papua New Guinea*. Fort Worth: Harcourt Brace Jovanovich.

INDEX